D1647009

a great deal of time, so this guidebook tries to be concise . . .

and I hope you will allow me to guide you around th.:

Welcome to Oxford, I am the Oxford Dodo

But before we get going, I just wanted to spend a moment pondering time. You have, after all, decided to spend a certain amount of it in Oxford, so I think it best to establish exactly what it is we are talking about.

Time can be hard to define; indeed one part of Oxford still keeps its own time. Until the mid-19th century each town and city followed local time, which was determined by the average position of the midday sun shining overhead, but this all changed with the introduction of the railway and the accompanying telegraph system. At Oxford (longitude 1 degree 15 minutes west of the Greenwich Meridian in London) the midday sun arrives five minutes later than in London.

One of Oxford's most famous colleges, Christ Church, has never quite got around to adopting this standard in full. It still holds services in the Cathedral by local Oxford time, and a college tradition says that you can only be late for meetings by Oxford time, thereby giving an extra five minutes grace. And if you hear Tom Tower tolling at five minutes past nine standard time, it's in commemoration of the college's nine o'clock curfew (see page 23).

Lewis Carroll, the author of the famous children's story *Alice's Adventures in Wonderland* published in 1865, was a don at Christ Church. The story begins with Alice following a white rabbit as he hurries along constantly muttering to himself 'Oh dear! Oh dear! I shall be so late!' So perhaps we should begin our book.

Oh yes, and you should visit the Museum of the History of Science to see its fascinating collection of devices which sometimes aided time keeping, such as this astrolobe from about 1370. ✑☞

The Dodo Guide to
OXFORD

Philip Atkins &
Michael Johnson

DODO PUBLISHING

4

Don't feel you need to read the boring bit
below, unless you are a bookseller, librarian,
or Ms Carryl Allardice BA, H, Dip.Lib., BA HONS,
MA, MBA, FCILIP, who is the London based
agent who requests publishers to supply the
free legal deposit copies for the libraries of
the University of Oxford, the University of
Cambridge, the National Library of Scotland,
the Library of Trinity College, Dublin, and
the National Library of Wales. The British
Library must also be sent a copy within
one month of publication; all of this is done under the provisions of the Legal Deposit Libraries Act 2003, chapter 28, section 1 (1) which replaced the Copyright Act...

Published and distributed by Dodo Publishing,
15 Pumbro, Stonesfield, Oxfordshire, OX29 8QF

First edition 2005 (otherwise Chinese year of the Fowl,
Muslim year AH 1426, or Jewish year AM 5765)
Copyright © Philip Atkins and Michael Johnson 2005

ISBN 0 9534438 1 7, 978 0 9534438 1 9

2

XI   XII

X

XIII

IX

Written, designed,
illustrated, and typeset by
the authors. Typeset in the Darjeeling
and Gantok typefaces © Michael Johnson.

Printed in the United Kingdom by
T. J. International Ltd,
Padstow, Cornwall

II

Whilst every
effort has been made
to ensure the accuracy of
the information contained in this
book, inevitably an occasional error or
omission will be present. Information on such
things as opening hours, and admission prices
regularly change. We cannot be held liable, but
would appreciate being informed.

VIII

III

This guidebook is an introduction to Oxford. We've selected some of the best colleges and buildings of the University, as well as museums, green spaces, and helpful hints on subjects such as literary Oxford and punting. Don't forget to stroll around its streets and lanes to take in the atmosphere of this great city—why not try the Dodo Walk (page 84)?

If you only have **a few hours** available, we suggest that you visit the grandest college, Christ Church (page 20), then walk to Carfax (the centre of the city) and down the High Street to relax in the Botanic Garden (page 60), with the option of a punting trip from nearby Magdalen Bridge.

For those with **a day or more** in Oxford it's well worth taking in the academic heart of the University situated around Radcliffe Square, by visiting the Bodleian Library (page 48), and a nearby college such as Brasenose (page 30).

If you have more time, or want to decide your own itinerary, then look through the list of contents on the next page to choose from the many treats available. There are sections devoted to the colleges, university buildings, museums, and general information.

At the back of this guidebook are various **maps** to help get you into Oxford and around the city centre. There are coach and railway stations, as well as a good Park & Ride bus system, to save you the headache of trying to park in the city centre.

A brief word from the Oxford Dodo

Time and tide wait for no man, not even a dodo, so let me introduce myself a little before this guidebook really gets under way.

My ancestors came from the island of Mauritius in the Indian Ocean. We were a contented lot in our island paradise, until a group of hungry Dutch sailors first sighted us in 1598. Within eighty years the rats, pigs, and monkeys they brought to the island caused our extinction. The Portuguese had the audacity to name us *valghvogel*, which translates as 'disgusting bird', after they tried to eat us.

You may be familiar with the phrase 'as dead as a dodo', but as you can see I'm not dead, deceased, or pushing up the daisies from six foot under. I haven't gone for a burton, bitten the dust, or snuffed it. Spiritually speaking I'm quite well thank you, at least nothing a nice cup of tea wouldn't sort out.

Well, how did I end up in Oxford, you may ask? I was one of the few dodos that was brought back across the seas to be exhibited in Europe. In 1638 Sir Hamon Lestrange reported seeing a dodo in an upstairs room in London, where its keeper fed it pebbles 'conducing to digestion' (at least that's what he said). After I died,

I suffered the humiliation of becoming an exhibit in Mr Tradescant's Ark of Curiosities in Lambeth, and from there I was moved to Oxford.

For a century I was gawped at by all and sundry who visited the Ashmolean Museum. I was then put in a cupboard for several years, so that by the mid-19th century only my skinny head with a few fine feathers and a foot survived (my spirit has risen above such minor setbacks).

I hope you have an enjoyable visit.

signed with a footprint[1]
Raphus cucullatus
(oxoniensis)

---

[1] please note, footprint, not footnote. Also, you can see my unique remains, including the foot itself (the sole surviving) in the Oxford University Museum of Natural History, Parks Road, in north Oxford (see page 69).

Contents

Just as Alice drank a bottle with a label that said 'DRINK ME', and ate a very small cake on which the words 'EAT ME' were beautifully marked in currants, so I suggest you read the following A to Z introduction to Oxford. By the end of it you should have metamorphosed into an expert on Oxford.

 is for King **Alfred**, who was supposed to have founded the University of Oxford in the year 800 and something. Or it might have been a more ancient king, **Argivarus**, or a monk named **Agricola**, or possibly a different monk named **Asser**. All of this is **apocryphal**. What we do know is that by **Anglo-Saxon** times there was a thriving settlement at the confluence of the rivers Thames and Cherwell, where oxen could cross at a ford— hence the name. The Normans built a castle, of which one tower and a big grassy mound can still be seen from New Road. The whole site, incorporating the later Oxford Prison, is being redeveloped with a hotel, restaurants, heritage centre, a market, and apartments.

is for **buses**. A good introduction to the city is to travel in comfort around its streets on board one of the open-top buses. This will help you get your bearings before exploring on foot. It's also for **Oxford Brookes University**, the city's other university (since 1992) with about 17,000 students. Roger **Bannister** was the first man to run a mile in under four minutes and he did it in Oxford in May 1954. Oxford is best looked at in a more leisurely way. Catch the bus tours at the stop opposite **Blackwell's**, one of the best **bookshops** in the world, on **Broad** Street.

C is for **colleges**. These are what you've come to see. They are the self-governing bodies where students study, founded from the 13th century onwards, that together make up the University. They are scattered throughout the city, their buildings intermingled with and adjoining each other in a way that for the visitor can be extremely **confusing**.

D is for **dictionary**. One of the things Oxford is famous for throughout the world is the Oxford English Dictionary, a stupendous enterprise begun in 1858, involving hundreds of researchers and thousands of **definitions**. Oxford University Press publish the dictionary and its many offspring, and have a small museum in their building in Great Clarendon Street (see page 71). D is also for **degrees**, the qualification all students aspire to, in which effort they are tutored by **dons**. It is of course also for our friend and guide the **dodo**, mistakenly defined by the above mentioned publication as extinct.

E is for **examinations**. If you see students wearing academic dress (short gowns, dicky-bows) and doomed expressions, they are probably on their way to the intimidating **Examination Schools** in the High Street. More relaxed students are likely to be on their way to the Sheldonian Theatre in Broad Street to have their degrees conferred upon them. E is also for **Eights**, one of the mysterious Oxford boat races and for **elevens** a traditional mid-morning break for food and drink.

F is for **Fellows**, senior members of a college with rights to vote on all issues and administrative duties to perform. There are various kinds of Fellow: Honorary Fellow, Emeritus Fellow, Supernumerary Fellow, and Young-Fellow-me-lad. Fellows are dons*.

a poorly defined dodo

An A–Z of Oxford

* In Christ Church, Fellows are called Students, with a capital 'S'.

G is for **guides**. This book is an example of one. But if the Dodo isn't a good enough guide for you and you want to have the services of a living, human guide, there are tours that set off from the gates at Trinity College and the Oxford Information Centre, both in Broad Street. G is also for **Greats**, the final part of the honours course in Classics, Philosophy, and Ancient History. **Great Tom** is Oxford's loudest bell, booming out one hundred and one times every evening at five minutes past nine from the tower at Christ Church, to commemorate the original number of its scholars. **Grotesques** are the disturbing or comic figures carved high up on many college buildings.

H is for **Sherlock Holmes**, the great detective, believed to have attended the University. In one of the stories he tells Doctor Watson that he was bitten on his ankle one morning as he was on his way to his college chapel. But which college did he attend? The **High Street**, sometimes referred to familiarly as 'The High', is of course one of the most beautiful streets in the world. It's also quite long. To give an idea of this, a kindly person (Dutch in this case) took 12 minutes and 12 seconds to walk from the far end of Magdalen Bridge to Carfax, in 1229 paces. He moved briskly, waiting a minute at a traffic light which had turned red, and allowed for no distractions (architectural, historical, or anthropological).

I is for **inaccessible**, as, unfortunately for the visitor, much of Oxford will prove to be. Some places may be accessible, but at **inconvenient** times. This will prove a delightful experience for everyone who enjoys being teased. The local name for the River Thames as it passes through Oxford is the **River Isis**. The origin of this name was first recorded in the 14th century and refers to the length of river upstream from Dorchester, where the River Thame joins it (note 'Thame', not 'Thames').

is for **Jericho**, one of Oxford's earliest suburbs, to the north west of the centre, laid out in a grid of small terraced brick houses occupied at first mostly by employees of Oxford University Press. Much of it is still there, having escaped post-war redevelopment.

is for **kings**. Richard the Lionheart and John were born in Oxford in a palace built for Henry I; Henry III built the city walls; Henry VIII brought Katherine of Aragon to the fertility well at Binsey to encourage the chances of a male heir; Charles I made the city his military headquarters for almost four years of the Civil War and was refused the loan of a book by the Bodleian Library; Charles II moved his court and parliament to Oxford in 1665 to avoid the plague of London; James VI and I* declared that if he were not a king he'd be an Oxford scholar; James II was successfully defied by Magdalen College when he tried to impose a Catholic principal and fellows on the college; William of Orange was given a feast, but ate almost nothing for fear of being poisoned and left early; George V was discovered on his knees next to the President of St John's, sticking stamps into an album; George VI broke the key as he was officially opening the New Bodleian Library; and Edward VIII was at Magdalen and a member of Vincent's, a club for sporty types.

 is for **Latin**, a good working knowledge of which will be invaluable for reading the countless inscriptions. Take the opportunity of your visit to learn this noble and ancient language and *uno slatu duos apros capere*, though the Dodo does not wish you to take this literally; he is, after all, your *vade mecum*. The great **lexicographer**, Samuel Johnson, was a student of Pembroke College from 1728, and had so little money that his toes stuck out of his worn boots.

An A–Z of Oxford

* For anyone unfamiliar with this strange looking title, king James (the only son of Mary, queen of Scots) was crowned king James VI of Scotland soon after his first birthday in 1567, and king James I of England in 1603.

M is for **Magdalen College**, always to be pronounced 'Mawd-lin', and for **Inspector Morse**, who discovered in the course of the novels written by Colin Dexter that Oxford has a startlingly high murder rate. Two very different men named **William Morris** have left their mark on Oxford. The first was the bearded Victorian poet, novelist, painter, designer, and early socialist, influential in his time, but leaving only some faded fresco marks, made with his Pre-Raphaelite friends in the Oxford Union. There's more to see at his home, **Kelmscott Manor**, near Lechlade. The other William Morris was the motor car manufacturer, later Viscount Nuffield, who became the city's largest employer and greatest benefactor.

☞
Unfortunately we are running short of space, but wanted to add that M is also for **Mensa** (an international organization for people good at IQ tests) which was founded by two barristers in 1946 in St John Street, Oxford.

N is for **North Oxford**, the leafy suburb of tall red and yellow brick Victorian houses, a delightful place to wander away from the crowds, especially in the spring and summer. It's also for the **Norrington Table**, published each year and showing which colleges have done best in the finals, a first-class degree scoring five points, an upper-second three points, etc.

O is also for the charity **Oxfam**, which grew out of the Oxford Committee for Famine Relief, founded in 1942. Its first shop opened in Broad Street and there are now over eight hundred.
☞

O is for Oxford's heraldic beast, the **Ox**, portrayed on the city arms high-stepping through the wavy waters of the ford. It's also for all things **Oxford**, from **Oxford English**—the approved way of speaking and writing, to **Oxford bags**—lavishly wide-bottomed trousers, fashionable among students in the 1920s, **Oxford sausages**, **Oxford marmalade**, **Oxford shoes**, **Oxford blue**, and the **Oxford comma**.

OXENFORD

(an Oxford comma, in the wild, as it were)

P is for **porters**, those vigilant, informative gatekeepers of the colleges. From the security of their lodges they will direct or frustrate your visit. Also for **Parson's Pleasure**, the bathing place on the River Cherwell where men only used to bathe and sunbathe in the nude.

is for **quadrangles**, those enclosed areas of Oxford colleges usually laid with immaculately shaven lawns that must never be set foot upon. The earliest quad at Merton College (see page 38) seems to have been formed by piecemeal development over time and then copied by later colleges. It is best to walk around in a clockwise direction. Gardeners are always grateful to hear of any dandelion or other weed that may have eluded their attentions.

is for the great many **riots** during Medieval times, with students fighting amongst themselves or against the citizens. Most infamous was a three-day pitched battle beginning on St Scholastica's Day 1355, sparked by an argument between students and an innkeeper over the quality of his wine. Many fatalities resulted, and for five hundred years the Mayor was made to swear an annual oath to observe the University's privileges. It is also for **Real Tennis**, an ancient indoor game played with rackets and a net, making cunning use of the surrounding walls. Merton College has the country's second oldest court still in use.

is for the **Oxford Story** in Broad Street, an excellent and unusual introduction to the city. It's a kind of sedate, spirally roller-coaster ride past recreated episodes of university history with a recorded guide. And it's for **St Giles**, a seventh-century hermit of Provence, patron saint of the poor and crippled, whose name was given to the broad street (broader than Broad Street) running northwards out of the city. It's the bizarre scene of the vast annual fair, traditionally held on the Monday and Tuesday following the first Sunday after St Giles' Day, 1 September. There are 162 churches dedicated to St Giles in England, including the one at the northern end of this street. The fair, first celebrated in 1634, was formerly a parish wake, but is now a funfair, and is well worth seeing.

An A–Z of Oxford

The Oxford
Information
Centre (telephone
01865 726871)
is included in a
useful website run
by Oxford City
Council:
www.visitoxford.org

Other sites to try:
www.dailyinfo.co.uk
www.ox.ac.uk
www.oxford.gov.uk
www.oxfordcity.co.uk
www.oxfordshire.co.uk
www.oxfordshire.gov.uk

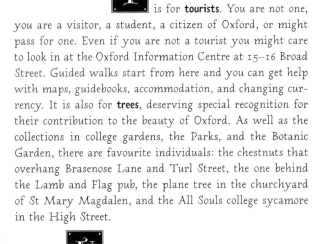

is for **tourists**. You are not one, you are a visitor, a student, a citizen of Oxford, or might pass for one. Even if you are not a tourist you might care to look in at the Oxford Information Centre at 15–16 Broad Street. Guided walks start from here and you can get help with maps, guidebooks, accommodation, and changing currency. It is also for **trees**, deserving special recognition for their contribution to the beauty of Oxford. As well as the collections in college gardens, the Parks, and the Botanic Garden, there are favourite individuals: the chestnuts that overhang Brasenose Lane and Turl Street, the one behind the Lamb and Flag pub, the plane tree in the churchyard of St Mary Magdalen, and the All Souls college sycamore in the High Street.

is for the **Union**, a student society founded in 1825 for debating in the English Parliamentary style. Past officers have included many distinguished men and women, including five Prime Ministers. Politicians and other celebrities from all over the world regularly visit to take part in debates. The most controversial was in 1933 when the motion was 'that this house will in no circumstances fight for its King and Country' which was carried by 275 votes to 153. And it's for **Up**. Wherever students start out from, this is the state they are in when they begin their Oxford term.

is for **viewpoints**. Get the bigger picture, with or without a camera, from the top of a tower, assuming you are fit enough for the stairs. The cupola of the Sheldonian Theatre (see page 54) is relatively easy, enclosed, and spacious. The spire of St Mary's Church (see page 58) is a tougher, more confined ascent and perhaps not for those prone to vertigo. Carfax Tower is all that's left of St Martin's Church and commands views of the towny side of Oxford, as does the Saxon tower of St Michael in

Cornmarket, and neither are particularly high. If you want the distant romantic view of spires and towers, you'll have to go to Headington Hill Park, or Boar's Hill.

 is for **William Wordsworth**, a Cambridge man, who addressed Oxford in one of his poems thus: 'Ye sacred Nurseries of blooming youth'! And for **women**, a relatively recent introduction to Oxford. Lady Margaret Hall and Somerville were the earliest women's halls, founded in the 1870s. However, women were not awarded degrees until 1920, and until 1957 the University imposed a limit on the number of women undergraduates. Oriel was the last college to admit women, in 1984.

marks the cross in the road surface of Broad Street close to where Archbishop Cranmer and Bishops Latimer and Ridley were burned at the stake for their supposed Protestant heresies.

—it's getting difficult now— is for the **Youth Hostel** right by the railway station in Botley Road. You don't have to be young to take advantage of this cheaper kind of accommodation.

and finally is for, well, **zoos**. The nearest is the Cotswold Wildlife Park, 29 kilometres (18 miles) west of Oxford. **Zebra crossings**, in case you are unfamiliar with them, are striped ways across roads where traffic is supposed to give way to pedestrians. And **Zacharias and Co.**, tailors and outfitters, manufacturers of all kinds of waterproof clothing—'Zacs for Macs'—closed its Cornmarket shop, alas, in 1983. And for **Zuleika Dobson**, perhaps the best novel about Oxford, written by Max Beerbohm in 1911.

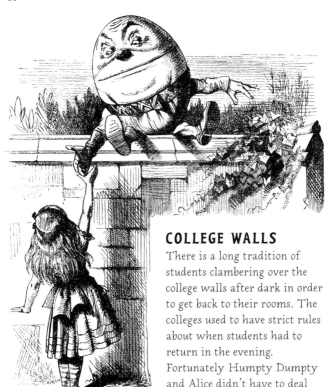

COLLEGE WALLS

There is a long tradition of students clambering over the college walls after dark in order to get back to their rooms. The colleges used to have strict rules about when students had to return in the evening. Fortunately Humpty Dumpty and Alice didn't have to deal with the barbed wire now usually present.

GROTESQUES

You will be watched wherever you go by an army of ugly faces high on college buildings. This Medieval custom of decorating Christian buildings has been perpetuated by generations of Oxford masons. Only heads with rain-spouts are true gargoyles (from the Old French *gargouille*, meaning throat).

Oxford University's colleges

Oxford University is a confederation of all its colleges, each of which is self governing, a small world unto itself where its students eat, sleep, and meet their tutors. The University is the overall authoritative and administrative body, organising curricula, the libraries, laboratories, examinations, managing finances and property, and conferring degrees. Its parliament is called Congregation, while legislation is proposed by the Council of the University (which recently replaced the grandly named Hebdomadal—that is Latin for weekly—Council).

Many colleges have features such as quadrangles, gatehouses, and gardens in common, so these are described overleaf. This is followed by seven colleges we think are particularly worth a visit. First amongst these is Christ Church which is probably Oxford's most famous and impressive college (it even incorporates Oxford Cathedral).

a typical college . . .

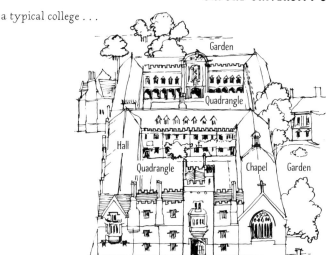

Garden

Quadrangle

Hall

Quadrangle   Chapel   Garden

Gatehouse, with
Porter's Lodge beneath

GATEHOUSES The entrance to many of the older colleges is signalled by a castellated tower with large wooden doors, a symbol of defence dating back to the times of pitched battles between town and gown. The heads of colleges often had their rooms over the entrance to keep an eye on the comings and goings of their charges. Within the gatehouse are noticeboards advertising the myriad formal and informal activities of the college, providing a flavour of its daily life.

PORTER'S LODGES are the enclosed cubby holes just inside the gatehouse, from where the porter, a kind of guardian and concierge, greets guests, supervises messages and mail, surveys the movements of members of the college, and suspicious aliens like yourself.

COLLEGE
CLOSED
*for no
particular
reason*

QUADRANGLES grew out of the courtyards of Medieval castles and palaces. Mob Quad at Merton, begun in 1287, was the first appearance of the characteristic tidy rectangular arrangement, usually housing student bedrooms and study cubicles, library, hall, and chapel. The rooms are off staircases approached from the quad via a lobby where occupants' names are displayed on a board. Buildings are of limestone, originally rough locally quarried stone but patched and replaced by more durable varieties over the centuries. Quads didn't always have manicured grass at their centre. Some had stone slabs or cobbles, others flower gardens and statues.

You may see colourful heraldry chalked on college walls. This celebrates achievements in the annual boat races, listing the vanquished or 'bumped' crews of other colleges.

THE CHAPEL Uniquely in Oxford the older chapels are T-shaped, entered by an antechapel, used in Medieval times for extra altars, where the walls are lined by memorials. The chapel itself is beyond a wooden screen, its seats arranged longitudinally so that choir and scholars could face each other to aid the responsive Medieval singing style. Above the altar is often an elaborate wall of statues in decorative niches, called a reredos, and sometimes a painting. A brass eagle lectern, wood panelling, an organ, stained glass, and a wooden beamed roof are often in evidence, some original, some restored or replaced.

THE HALL has rows of dark paintings of college dignitaries hanging on dark panelled walls and an aroma of cooking hangs in the air. Open fireplaces in the middle of the floor and holes in the roof for escaping smoke are gone, but the arrangement is still that of a Medieval nobleman's hall, with tables and benches, a raised dais at one end for high table, and a carved wooden screen at the other to hide the ways to kitchen, buttery, and pantry.

GARDENS From Medieval times the colleges had their herb and vegetable plots, orchards, and walks. After the Renaissance some fashionable ideas from the continent— fountains, statues, ornamental flowerbeds, topiary — were briefly tried. Dominant today is the English Landscape Garden style of the 18th and 19th centuries, with its park-like lawns, specimen trees, informal shrubberies, and winding paths.

① Christk Church and Oxford Cathedral

Christ Church is a place of superlatives. The biggest quad, the biggest hall, the biggest library, its own art gallery, Oxford's cathedral for its chapel, the biggest gate tower with the loudest bell, and it has educated thirteen of the country's prime ministers.

*

OPENING TIMES
9.30am–5.30pm
Monday–Saturday,
and 11.30am–5.30pm
Sunday. Admission
charge.

ENTRANCE
from St Aldate's, then
Broad Walk.

see map ➡ D4

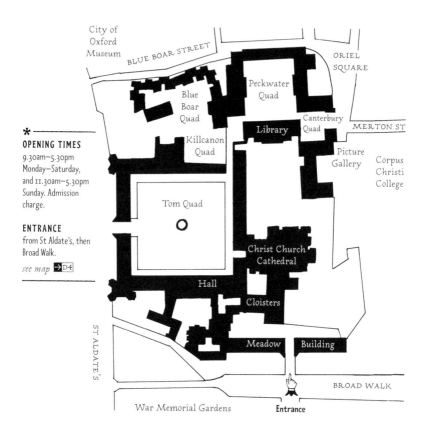

You will probably approach Christ Church along St Aldate's and try to enter by the big gate under Tom Tower. If you do, a bowler-hatted custodian will politely redirect you to the visitors' entrance from the Broad Walk. But before being moved on, admire **Tom Tower** from the other side of the road. The college was founded by Cardinal Wolsey in 1525, but was barely begun by the time of his disgrace and downfall four years later. So what we see is a wall and lower part of the tower that is Wolsey's work, and a top part, the domed tower, added in a much simpler style by Sir Christopher Wren in 1682, making one of the memorable features of the Oxford skyline. There is a statue of Wolsey in a niche at the centre of the big window over the gateway.

Wren's Tom Tower as viewed from St Aldate's.

Carry on down St Aldate's and turn left into the War Memorial Gardens, laid out in 1925. Straight ahead is the Broad Walk, saved from a plan to turn it into an inner relief road after the Second World War. It was once lined with tall elms, sadly lost to disease in the 1970s and now replanted with lime. To the right the Poplar Walk leads towards the river. We enter the college through **Meadow Buildings** (1862), a grim hulk of Victorian Gothic, though the views of Christ Church Meadow from the students' windows must make up for that.

Follow the signs from the entrance to the **Cloister**. This was originally part of St Frideswide's Priory, founded in the 12th century to house the relics of the saint. After the Dissolution of the Monasteries ordered by Henry VIII, the priory was cannibalised by Cardinal Wolsey for his new college. He made the priory church his college chapel and later it became the cathedral of the diocese of Oxford.

Since becoming famous, Alice and her friends are often troubled by tourists.

The man in the paper hat is John Tenniel's caricature of Benjamin Disraeli, who later became prime minister (1868, and 1874–1880).

Follow directions round the Cloister and towards the **Hall**, approached by a grand staircase. Above it fan vaulting sprays out from a single tall slender column. It looks Medieval, but like Tom Tower, it was built in the 17th century, and the staircase itself in 1805. It featured in the recent Harry Potter films and has become a favourite photo-opportunity.

At the top of the stairs, pass through the Ante Hall into the **Dining Hall**, a vast space made dark by the wood of the hammerbeam roof, the wall panelling, and the backgrounds of the many portraits of famous members of the college. The room dates from Wolsey's time. At the far end is High Table, where the dons dine. Lovers of the Alice books can see portraits of her and other characters in the fifth window along on the left hand side of the hall, and her telescopic neck may have been inspired by the brass firedogs in the fireplaces. An inconspicuous doorway in the wall behind High Table was the hole down which the Dean—or White Rabbit—vanished after dinner. A portrait of Lewis Carroll (his real name was Charles Dodgson), the author of the books, can be seen near the entrance door. He taught mathematics at Christ Church for many years.

Go back down the stairs to enter **Tom Quad**, passing political graffiti of 1829, the words 'No Peel' hammered into a door by students protesting at reforms by the Home Secretary Sir Robert Peel, a Christ Church man. Tom Quad was meant to be a cloister quad like Magdalen's, part of Cardinal Wolsey's ambitious foundation of 1525 after the dissolution of St Frideswide's Priory, but Wolsey fell and the side roofs were never built. The Quad is dominated by Sir Christopher Wren's tower built in 1682 to complete the gatehouse. Tom Tower houses Great Tom, a seven ton bell cast in 1680. Each evening at five minutes past nine, not nine o'clock because Oxford is 1 degree and 15 minutes west of the Greenwich Meridian in London, it tolls 101 times, once for every member of the original college foundation. It was muffled in 1965 for the passage through Oxford of the body of Churchill on its way to be buried at Bladon, near Woodstock. Mercury has stood on tiptoe over the fish pond since 1928. One morning in the 1950s a swan was discovered in the pond in Tom Quad wearing a black bow tie.

Enter the **Cathedral** from the Quad. A helpful free plan available inside suggests a clockwise route. Follow the same route to take in our selection of highlights:

• The Jonah window by Abraham van Linge, 1630s. A brilliantly coloured mixture of stained and painted glass, the only window to survive Protestant disfavour from a set of thirteen. Fragments of others were recently discovered in an old college coal-hole.

• St Frideswide's shrine in the Latin Chapel, 13th century, smashed on the orders of Henry VIII, reassembled in the 19th century from pieces found in an old well, and restored and reconstructed again in 2002. Good carvings of faces peering from leaves. Alongside a watching loft, with an open wooden top, for keeping guard on the shrine, and a big window by the Pre-Raphaelite artist Edward Burne-Jones (1858) showing scenes of St Frideswide's life, its violent colours in contrast to those of Medieval windows nearby.

St Frideswide is the patron saint of Oxford and the University, about whom little is known except that she died in the 8th century after founding a religious house. Her name means 'bond of peace'. In the cathedral and cloister and on her shrine you will see carvings of a woman's face peering through leaves, a memory of when she hid in the woods from a persistent suitor and lived with swineherds.

Christ Church's coat of arms featuring Wolsey's hat with fashionable tassles, or is it a flying saucer with elaborate feeding system?

• Enjoyable tombs leading into The Lady Chapel. Look out for the giant John de Nowers with a white nose, his head pillowed on an ox-head helmet. Above him is a wall monument to Robert Burton, student at Christ Church and author of *The Anatomy of Melancholy*, named here as Democritus. Suitably grim, he is framed by an astrological sign and his horoscope, which correctly predicted his death to within an hour.

• Look up from in front of the altar at the lovely, intricate stone vaulting, patterned in star-shapes, probably by William Orchard, the designer of the similar roof in the Divinity School (see Bodleian Library, page 48).

• In the Lucy Chapel more wonderful stained glass, this time 14th-century, one panel showing Thomas Becket kneeling between a monk and the knights who are about to murder him.

Leave the cathedral by the door into the cloister, where you can turn to the left and visit the video room or the Chapter House (entered by a fine Norman doorway) which has become the Cathedral shop, also displaying college gold and silver plate.

Return to Tom Quad and proceed to **Killcanon Quad**, passing under Fell Tower, which like Bell Tower on the Hall side of Tom Quad, is a sympathetic Victorian addition. Killcanon is a diminutive quadrangle, built in the 1670s, with a sundial high on one wall, and leads into **Peckwater Quad**. This is big and rigorously Classical. Three of its sides are identical, designed by Henry Aldrich, dean of the college, and completed in 1714, while the fourth side is the detached **Library**, not completed until 1772. This was designed by Dr George Clarke, Fellow of All Souls, lawyer, politician, and talented amateur architect, and is on a monumental scale, with Corinthian columns of enormous girth. Unusually it is built of two contrasting colours of stone, white Portland, and creamy Clipsham. The ground floor was originally designed to be an open arcade, but was soon enclosed to make space for a picture gallery, the library itself remaining on the upper floor. The interior decoration is beautiful, but alas there is no public access.

The Canterbury Gate in Oriel Square shown in this 19th-century wood engraving, by the illustrious Mr Orlando Jewitt.

Your tour of the college ends with **Canterbury Quad**, built in 1783 by James Wyatt, in harmony with the look of Peckwater Quad, but on a more modest scale, except for the Roman triumphal arch onto Merton Street and Oriel Square. If you'd like to stay longer, you can visit the college **Picture Gallery**, cunningly fitted in during the 1960s and entered by an unobtrusive doorway in Canterbury Quad. It's an impressive and enjoyable collection of Old Master paintings and drawings, often hosting temporary exhibitions.

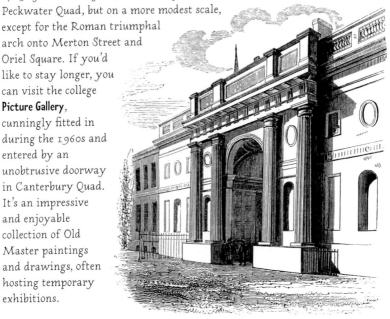

② Magdalen College

𝔄 college made memorable by its sylvan setting of river, water meadows, gardens, and deer park. It was founded in 1458, with a President, forty Fellows, thirty Scholars, eight Clerks, and sixteen Choristers. Today there are six hundred students and seventy-five Fellows, but Magdalen is still pronounced 'mawd-lin', as it was five hundred years ago. Its bell tower beside Magdalen Bridge seems to signal the entrance to the heart of Oxford for travellers approaching from London.

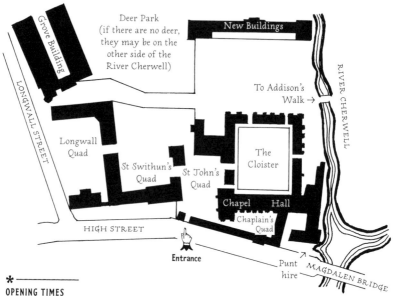

* ─────────

OPENING TIMES
1 October to 27 June: 1pm–6pm, or dusk
28 June to 30 September: 12pm–6pm
Admission charge
Visitor's shop
The Old Kitchen Bar

ENTRANCE
from the High Street.
see map **→** F3

Enter from the High Street by the **Gatehouse** after admiring the famous and beautiful **Bell Tower**, completed in 1509 and refaced in stone in the 1970s. It is 144 feet or 44 metres high, quite plain in its lower stages to set off its decorative crown of pierced parapets and pinnacles. At dawn on May Day the college choir sing a Latin anthem from the top, bells are rung, followed by Morris dancing, champagne breakfasts, and other boisterous activities across the city.

The first quadrangle you enter is **St John's**. In the corner to your right is a small stone pulpit from which the University sermon is preached on St John the Baptist's Day (24 June). The hospital of St John the Baptist, tending to the sick and weary travellers, was here from 1180 until the college closed it down with royal permission in 1485. Ahead are the President's Lodgings (1888), and next to it the old Grammar Hall (1614), with a tiny bell turret, where choristers were taught Latin, perhaps to prepare them for entrance to the college. To the left of these are St Swithun's Buildings (1884). All are private. Before leaving St John's Quadrangle you might like to look into **Chaplain's Quadrangle**, a little triangular left-over space between buildings, with a garden and a modern sculpture of Christ and St Mary Magdalen. Look up to see the parade of grotesque carved creatures, with some quite normal-looking characters, perhaps Magdalen dons, keeping them company.

Return to St John's Quad, where the most interesting sight, which we have ignored so far, is the large west doorway of the **Chapel** (finished 1480), decorated with battlements and statues. But you can't enter the chapel this way, you must go beneath the Muniment Tower, the not-very-high tower next to the chapel (the Founder's Tower is the taller one further along that was originally the entrance to the college) and turn right.

Martin Routh (1755–1854) became college President at the age of 35 and held office until he died in his hundredth year, wearing his wig till the end and refusing to acknowledge the existence of railways. Stories of him abound, including:

DON: President! something appalling has happened. One of the Fellows has killed himself.

ROUTH: Pray do not tell me who. Allow me to guess.

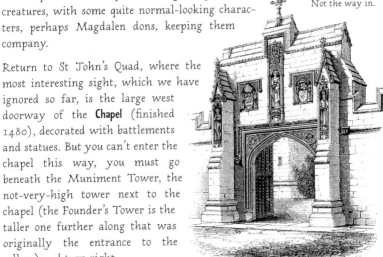

The Victorian gateway to the college from the High Street. Not the way in.

Muniments are archives, which the colleges traditionally kept in the upper floors of towers, for security.

Misericords are brackets on the underside of hinged choir stall seats, to support the weary during long periods of standing. Lift them to see the carvings.

Two of the monuments in the antechapel, to William Langton (1626) and Laurence Humphrey (1590) are in a Renaissance style you will see in many colleges— a coloured half-length figure looking out from a pulpit or window-like niche.

The chapel is built to the same T-shaped plan as other Oxford colleges, so that where you enter is the antechapel, the cross-bar of the T. As well as the unusual sepia-coloured 17th-century glass in the windows, there are interesting memorials, brasses, a copy of Leonardo da Vinci's Last Supper, and some surviving misericords with lively and sometimes irreverent carvings. Don't miss the delightful small backlit stained glass nativity window by John Piper. You cannot enter the chapel proper, but must peer through the screen under the organ. This, like most of the fittings, sculpture, and glass you see are Victorian, but faithful to Medieval ideals. If you wish to attend a sung service, these are held six days a week during term-time and the public are welcome.

Leave the chapel and turn right into the **Cloister**. Unlike the one at New College, made and used for burials, this is a combined cloister and quadrangle, with doors and steep steps leading up to sets of student rooms. Perched on the internal buttresses are large grotesques, called hieroglyphics—hippo, jester, greyhound, wrestlers (or perhaps they are dancers)—once painted in colours. A wide flight of steps leads up to the **Hall**. This has the usual college arrangements for dining, with the High Table for dons at the far end. The dark vertical pattern of linenfold panelling around the walls is original. Above High Table are carved panels (1541) depicting scenes from the life of St Mary Magdalen. One features Henry VIII. At the end you are viewing from the wood carving becomes more richly ornate, with Corinthian columns. A bust of Oscar Wilde, who was a student at Magdalen in the 1870s faces the fireplace from a window ledge near the centre of the room.

Take one of the passageways out of the cloister to see the long, low shape of **New Buildings** (1733), like an elongated Georgian country house. There were plans at the time to add two or three more sides to make a giant quadrangle connected to the cloister. It is an admirably undecorated, confident building, with an arcade on the ground floor where it is pleasant to dally, admiring the view back towards the bell tower. The Victorians did not admire the building, but thankfully never quite got round to their plan to 'Medievalize' it.

To the left is Magdalen Grove, where deer were first introduced in the late 17th century. The magnificent plane tree nearby was planted in 1801. Further in this direction you can see, but not enter, **Grove Building**, Magdalen's newest (begun in 1995), but not at all new-looking, building. It was designed by Dmitri Porphyrios, in a traditional style, which would surely be approved of by the Prince of Wales.

Through the gates and over the bridge eastwards is **Addison's Walk**, a circular path around the water meadows, a nature reserve where snake's head fritillary flowers in springtime. Addison, the 18th-century essayist, was a Fellow at Magdalen and a critic of formal gardening.

If you do complete the full circuit, one of the most pleasant walks in Oxford, you deserve to take a seat on the terrace of the Old Kitchen Bar (entered from the cloister) with a cup of tea and a slice of cake to watch the antics of novice punters setting out from under Magdalen Bridge.

Many famous people have had rooms in New Buildings, including John Betjeman (poet laureate), Addison, and Edward Gibbon (author of *The History of the Decline and Fall of the Roman Empire*), who described his time here as the most idle and unprofitable of his whole life.

There was once, reputedly, a disgraceful student custom of trying to get the deer drunk by dropping sugar lumps soaked in port from the windows of New Buildings.

③ Brasenose College

The only college entered directly from Radcliffe Square, it is a compact and delightful trio of quadrangles overlooked by the Radcliffe Camera's dome and St Mary's Church spire. Brasenose has been known at various times for its associations with north-west England and the Welsh border counties, the landed gentry, Puritanism, and for its sporting prowess, once fielding eight members of the University cricket team.

The hall contains the prized object that gives the college its odd name and seems to have led to a fascination with noses. Watch out for examples!

✳

OPENING TIMES
10–11.30am and 2–5pm in summer, or 2–4.30pm in winter. Please note that only groups are allowed to visit during the morning opening times, and individual visitors during the afternoon. Admission charge.

ENTRANCE
from Radcliffe Square, opposite the Radcliffe Camera

see map ➜ D3

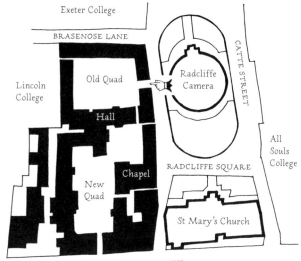

Exeter College

BRASENOSE LANE

Lincoln College

Old Quad

Hall

New Quad

Chapel

Radcliffe Camera

CATTE STREET

RADCLIFFE SQUARE

St Mary's Church

All Souls College

HIGH STREET

Before entering Brasenose College at its **Gatehouse** in Radcliffe Square take a moment to look at the Tudor royal arms over the entrance. At the apex of the original oak doors sits a tiny big-nosed head—our first brasenose.

Beneath the gatehouse pause a moment to adjust to the atmosphere of a different world, and enjoy the cornucopia of notices and posters, before proceeding into the Old Quad.

Apparently the Brasenose gatehouse is an example of a bombus, a sort of echo which answers to a particular note. Don't try it!

The **Old Quad** was completed along with the gatehouse in 1516 and it was all that there was of the college for 150 years. It was a compact, self-contained world which by 1552 had a college population of seventy, of whom forty-five were undergraduates. As an alternative to adding an extra floor the attics were converted into rooms called cock-lofts, lit by dormer windows; the last six cock-lofts were put in by an intriguingly named Oxford carpenter, Chrysostome Parkes.

The manicured lawn in the centre of the quad was once a low walled garden of clipped hedges and trees, a maze, and winding paths—like the pleasure garden of an Elizabethan manor. In 1727 it was levelled and a lead copy of Giovanni Bologna's *Samson Killing the Philistine* was set up. Familiarly referred to as *Cain and Abel*, the statue was regularly abused by the artistic and gymnastic students until it was sold for scrap in 1881.

This mid-19th-century engraving shows the Old Quadrangle, the copy of Bologna's statue, the gate tower (much too fat), and St Mary's Church spire in the distance.

W. A. DELAMOTTE, DEL

O. JEWITT SC.

Rooms around the quadrangle are arranged in vertical blocks served by a common staircase. The outer doors have the number of each staircase over them, with a list of the occupants just inside. Ground-floor rooms originally had earth or gravel floors, until they were 'boorded' in 1569. Even in 1596 they were referred to as 'dampeshe and unholsome'.

Over the **Hall Porch** are two crumbly heads, possibly King Alfred, once supposed to have founded the University, and Duns Scotus, the Medieval theologian and philosopher, who taught at Oxford. It is not clear who is who. Two other weathered heads are found higher up in niches on the parapet. These are the founders, William Smyth, Bishop of Lincoln, and Richard Sutton, a lawyer. Standing in the porch you can look back across the quad at the splendid sundial of 1719 and try to work out the time with the aid of the daunting diagram on the wall to your left, just inside the porch.

The **Hall** has always been the centre of college life, where members still eat together. Tables were originally arranged around a central hearth, the smoke escaping through the louvres in the roof lantern we saw from outside. The high table, reserved for senior members, is at the far end, raised on a not so very high dais, and lit by a bay window on either side. The high table end is topped by a dramatic Stuart royal coat of arms, with a particularly rampant lion and unicorn, and at the screen end are the college arms, scallop shells, and swags. Behind the high table is the Brasenose itself. This is the bronze ring handle or knocker of an ancient door, probably 12th- or early 13th-century. The story has it that a number of masters and scholars left Oxford in 1333 to get away from the noise and rioting, taking with them the door handle of Brasenose Hall and fixing it to a building in Stamford, Lincolnshire, where they resumed their studies. They were driven back to Oxford by royal command, but left their Brasenose behind. Five and a half centuries later the college, in possession of the site and name of Brasenose, but not the legendary knocker, heard that a Brasenose Hall in Stamford, lately a girls' school, was up for sale. The

The Brasenose represents a head that might be human, but is more likely to be a stylized lion or leopard. It possibly once formed part of the sanctuary door—to grab hold was to gain immunity from the law.

college bought the house in 1890 and carried the Brasenose in triumph back to Oxford, set it in a handsome frame, and stuck it as a trophy on the wall where you see it today. More big noses in the bay window looking into the quad.

Leave the hall and from the Old Quad there is a passage (called Dagg or Dog's Lane) in the south-east corner that leads to the pocket sized **Chapel Quad** of 1666, once jokingly nicknamed 'The Deer Park'. On the west side of the quad is the kitchen with its wonderful barley sugar chimneys. The kitchen is probably the oldest surviving part of the college, a remnant of an academic hall on this site before the foundation of the college. To the east is the library above the old cloister (later filled in for more rooms) with strange oval portholes.

In the 18th century John Osmond, a debauched MA of New Inn Hall, was expelled for biting off a piece of the nose of Thomas Greaves, BA of Brasenose, in a scuffle . . .

Enter the **Chapel**. It has remarkable fan-vaulting of plaster and wood fitted like a skin over a Medieval roof salvaged from another building. Hammer beams and pendants were left sticking through the fans. The Victorians added the dainty painted decorations.

The **New Quad** is the Victorian extension to the college, so it isn't really all that new after all. You can only look in, as it's private. Its best side is seen from the High Street.

The college's grandest face is its **High Street frontage**, but you will have to leave the college entirely and walk around past St Mary's Church and stand on the other side of the High Street to get the best view. Built between 1886 and 1911, to the designs of T. G. Jackson, it makes a fine show, although the grand doorway is rarely used. Here once again are the Oxford trademarks: square gate tower, gables, oriel windows, royal coat of arms, clustered chimneys, and decorative carving, all done with great gusto. Particularly enjoyable is the wealth of beautifully detailed carved foliage on the oriel parapets and all the swarming dragons, devils, angels, and beasts. It is tempting to start looking for Brasenoses—is that one wearing a mortar-board, or is it an ape? In fact if you look closely at the top of both doors you'll find them.

④ New College

A proudly anachronistic name for a place that's more than 600 years old. It was the first college to be designed around a quadrangle and on such a scale that it was larger than all the earlier colleges combined. It is said that its original cess-pit was so capacious that it didn't need to be emptied for 300 years.

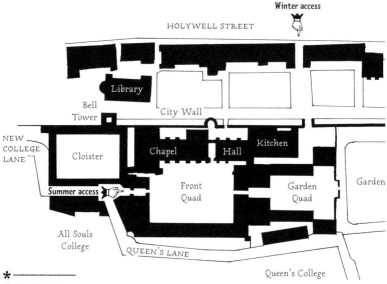

OPENING TIMES
Easter–October:
11am–5pm every day,
otherwise 2–4pm.
Admission charge in
summer.

ENTRANCE
from Holywell Street,
or New College Lane
(summer only).

see map → E3

The college is best approached along dog-legged and narrow New College Lane, from Catte Street. Pass between the blank walls of the cloisters on the left, and the college barn, which once held the produce of its country estates. The lane then turns sharp right under a 17th-century bridge joining the Warden's Lodgings to the college barn, but we go forward to enter the college by the **Gatehouse**, the first of its kind in Oxford. The rugged oak door is original. Above, the top floor has carvings of the Virgin flanked by a kneeling angel and the founder, William of Wykeham, Bishop of Winchester and Chancellor of England. At the same time he also founded a school at Winchester, expressly to supply his new college with properly trained students.

The **Front Quad** shows the ambitious size of the early college, complete by 1400 (the year of Chaucer's death), and the first to be built all in one go, for a warden, seventy scholars, ten chaplains, three clerks, and sixteen choristers. Chapel and Hall, joined end to end, make up the north side of the quad, with the four storey Muniment Tower at their far end. The new sundial on the tower is interpreted with the aid of a tablet on the wall of the gatehouse. The east side has the old library above and the bursary below, with a way through to the garden. The south side had bedrooms and study cubicles for students and Fellows, and the gatehouse

The approach to New College along New College Lane. The artist has disturbed one of the dons in an illicit assignation.

The coat of arms are those of the founder, William of Wykeham, defined as argent, two chevronels sable between three roses gules, seeded or, barbed vert.

Reynolds was as unimpressed with how his window turned out as we are likely to be. He put himself in it disguised as a shepherd—the one in the yellow smock looking over his shoulder. The surviving parts of the Medieval window were moved to York Minister.

side has the Warden's Lodgings. An additional storey was added on three sides in the 17th century, clearly shown by the change in stone, and sash windows were put in to replace the original stone mullioned and transomed windows.

The passageway from the north west corner of the quad leads to the **Chapel** entrance. First you enter the antechapel, the cross bar of the T-shaped plan. There is some wonderful surviving Medieval stained glass here, by one Thomas Glazier of Oxford, featuring saints, prophets, and angels in beautiful subtle colours. The big west window was replaced in 1788 by the only window ever designed by Joshua Reynolds. It is painted rather than stained glass. Standing beneath this window is Jacob Epstein's tortured figure of Lazarus (1951), still in his grave shrouds. There are 263 names on the Great War memorial carved by Eric Gill in 1921. He also did the much smaller memorial with the names of German members of the college who fought and died on the other side. Move through the organ screen (Victorian, though the doors are original and the organ above is uncompromisingly modern) into the Chapel proper. All the furnishings here are Victorian restoration except for the enjoyable Medieval choirstalls with carved elbow rests and misericords. The giant stone reredos behind the altar is a recreation of the Medieval one that was plastered over in the 18th century. Don't miss William of Wykeham's gorgeous crozier in a glass case near the altar, and the painting of St James by El Greco.

Beyond the Chapel entrance is the **Cloister**, built originally as a burial ground and used briefly as the main arsenal for the King's Army in the English Civil War. A lovely evergreen holm oak stands within it. Eight crumbling Medieval figures, deposed from the tower of St Mary's Church in the High Street during a restoration, haunt the gloom of the cloister. From here there is a good view of the college bell tower, built just after the cloister.

Return to the Front Quad and climb the steep steps at the foot of the Muniment Tower into the **Hall**. Notice the doorways leading off the passage to the Hall, leading to the kitchen, buttery, and pantry, one with carvings of boys carrying bread and beer. The Hall has Medieval linenfold panelling all around, a Victorian wooden roof based on the original, heraldic stained glass, and portraits.

From the Front Quad go into **Garden Quad**, 17th- and 18th-century extensions to the college that expand towards the beautiful wrought iron screen and gates of 1711 ('Manners Makyth Man' it says over them, so behave yourself), and which lead on to the **Garden** itself. This is bounded on two sides by one of the best-preserved stretches of the city wall (this section was built between 1226 and 1240). A condition of this land passing to the college was that the Mayor and Corporation would visit every three years to see that it was well maintained. The artificial mound, now covered with trees, was made in 1594 as a viewpoint from which to admire the clipped hedges and flower beds that were the style of the garden at that time. The mound originally had ornamental terraces and a gazebo on top.

William Spooner, sixty two years at New College and warden from 1903 to 1924, was prone to transposing the initial letters of words, for example: 'you have tasted two worms and hissed my mystery lectures'. The term Spoonerism appeared in the Oxford English Dictionary in his lifetime. He is also supposed to have asked a student 'Now let me see. Was it you or your brother who was killed in the war?'

The land that William of Wykeham bought up for New College and its garden was a plague burial area 'full of filth, dirt, and stinking carcasses...'

In the 19th century a noted view of the city walls, chapel, and bell tower, could be had from the 'slipe', a slip of ground at the back of the college that included the stables and other 'offices' (including what looks like a stonemason's workshop).

⑤ Merton College

One of the earliest colleges to be founded (in 1264)—disputing first place with Balliol and University—it set the early pace in Oxford by establishing the look for both quadrangles and chapels. In 1710 a grumpy German visitor named Z. C. von Uffenbach dismissed Merton as 'several ugly old buildings'.

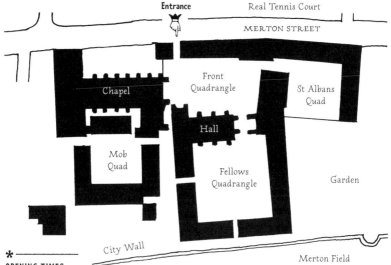

Entrance

Real Tennis Court

MERTON STREET

Chapel

Front Quadrangle

St Albans Quad

Hall

Mob Quad

Fellows Quadrangle

Garden

City Wall

Merton Field

OPENING TIMES
2–4pm Monday–Friday, and 10am–4pm Saturday–Sunday. Free admission. Tours are available July–September of the College (including the Old Library) for which there is a charge.

ENTRANCE
from Merton Street.

see map ➡ E4

Enter from Merton Street (the only surviving cobbled street in the city) through the **Gateway** begun in 1416 and completed sometime in the 1460s. The stone panel above the door shows the founder Walter de Merton, with John the Baptist, a unicorn, assorted woodland creatures, the Lamb of God, and the Book of Seven Seals from Revelation.

Now you are in **Front Quad**, the Hall straight ahead and the Chapel to your right. The chapel tower is one of the beauties of the city skyline, a kind of older (by fifty years) and stockier brother (or sister) to Magdalen's. The Hall is private, but look at the original oak door, decorated with fantastic tendrils of ironwork.

Go down the passage between Hall and Chapel and turn into **Mob Quad** (the name is a mystery). This was finished by 1378, the first complete Oxford quad, built in stages, so accidentally creating the now familiar enclosed arrangement that became the model for Oxbridge colleges. Along two sides of the top floor is the **Old Library**, marvellously preserved as it was at the end of Elizabeth's reign, and probably the oldest surviving working library in the United Kingdom. Fortunately for us it is the one college library that can be visited.

Leave the Quad by the passage opposite the one you entered Mob Quad by to find the door to the **Chapel**. Spacious as it seems, this is only a part of what was intended. The T-shape of the completed choir and transepts was copied in many later college chapels. Apart from the Medieval stained glass in the east window and in the side windows of the choir, look out for the wall monuments to Sir Henry Savile, attended by Ptolemy, Euclid, Tacitus, and St John Chrysostom, and to his friend Sir Thomas Bodley, founder of the Bodleian Library, who prefers the company of half-dressed allegorical ladies. There is also a surprising font of Siberian green jasper, given by the Tsar Alexander I in 1822.

Retrace your steps to the Front Quad and then go into the **Fellows' Quad**. This was built in 1610 by Warden Savile, the first quad in Oxford to go as high as three storeys. Its symmetry is broken on one side by an extravagant Tower of Orders, an early demonstration of the use of Classical columns and probably the inspiration for the even bigger tower at the Bodleian Library. Go through the passage under the tower for the rural view over the old city wall.

Lastly, we must mention the Merton Time Ceremony that marks the 'stand still' hour each autumn when clocks change from British Summer Time back to Greenwich Mean Time. College members, in full academic dress, link arms in groups of two or four, and solemnly walk backwards around Fellows' Quad. The ritual takes place between 2am and 3am, during which port is drunk. It is thought essential to the preservation of the regular passage of time and space.

A. C. Irvine, still an undergraduate at the time, died at or near the summit of Everest with Mallory in 1924. He practiced by clambering up and down the chapel walls.

Real tennis is the forerunner of modern lawn tennis, and shares the same scoring system. It can be played by two or four people. Service is always delivered from the same side of the court, into the 'hazard' side. A small solid ball is hit with rackets over the net, or off the side walls. Its origins can be traced to a game played in monastery cloisters in the 11th century, initially with a bare or gloved hand. Access to Merton's court is not normally possible, although a polite request may enable you to watch a game.

⑥ St John's College

With splendid architecture from the 15th to the 20th centuries and a lovely college garden, St John's is one of the sights in Oxford. Its frontage is shielded by a unique private buffer zone of earth and trees, looking ideal for a game of boule. A French family, no doubt feeling at home, were recently seen to set up a folding table and chairs there for a lavish picnic. The college wouldn't approve of either activity.

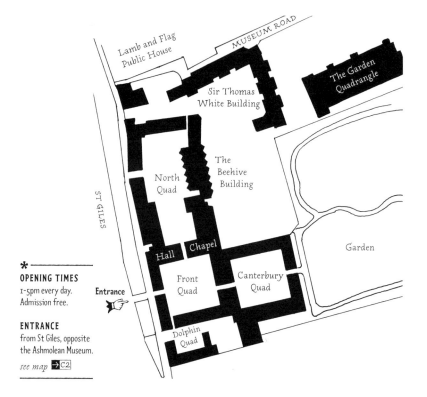

Lamb and Flag Public House

MUSEUM ROAD

The Garden Quadrangle

Sir Thomas White Building

The Beehive Building

North Quad

ST GILES

Hall   Chapel

Garden

Front Quad

Canterbury Quad

Entrance 👉

Dolphin Quad

✳ ─────
OPENING TIMES
1–5pm every day.
Admission free.

ENTRANCE
from St Giles, opposite
the Ashmolean Museum.

see map ➜ C2

Enter by the **Gatehouse** from St Giles through the original wooden doors, glancing up first at St Bernard on the top floor of the tower. When St John's was founded in 1555 it took over the buildings of St Bernard's, a Cistercian monastic college. Go into the **Front Quad**, still much as it was in the 15th century. To your left are the **Hall** and **Chapel**, divided by a passageway under the clock added in 1919. The Hall is not open to the public, but the Chapel is, entered from the passageway. It was thoroughly remodelled in Victorian times.

You can look into the **North Quad** from the end of the passage. Here are buildings of many periods, including Oxford's first brush with Modern architecture, the **Beehive Building** of 1960, hexagonal blocks of study bedrooms angled to the south west for the best light.

Return to the Front Quad. Opposite the Gatehouse are the President's lodgings and the passage to Canterbury Quad, both given elaborate carved door cases in 1633.

Canterbury Quad (1635) is a spectacular set piece from the years before the Civil War, a mixture of traditional Medieval college style (battlements, grotesque heads, gothic windows) and newly fashionable Renaissance architecture evident on two sides with arcades of columns, richly carved centrepieces, bronze statues of King Charles I and Queen Henrietta Maria, topped by curved pediments. Between the arcade columns are carved busts of ladies representing Geometry, Music, Fortitude, and Charity, amongst others.

Go through the archway to the **Garden**, noticing the original carved doors with strapwork ornament. The Garden is a lavish sweep of lawn and trees in the English landscape style of the 18th century. Bear left on entering to find, past the rock garden, St John's second post-war project, the Sir Thomas White Building (1975), unashamedly Modern. By the time of the Garden Quadrangle (1994) further along (both are private), there are post-Modern historical references in its brick towers, Classical proportions, and concrete made to look like stone. The gate in the garden wall has a lens set in it.

Canterbury Quad was the gift of William Laud, Archbishop of Canterbury under King Charles I, and Chancellor of the University. He is famous for his laws and statutes for all aspects of University life, including a complete ban on football. His feast to open the Quad was attended by the King, and cost £2,666 1s. 7d., half the cost of the building. Like his King, he lost his head in the Civil War.

The statue of St Bernard on the gatehouse facing St Giles was once disguised as John the Baptist by the addition of cement hair and beard. He became St Bernard again in 1915. On the Quad side is a real John the Baptist, carved by Eric Gill in 1936.

⑦ All Souls College

All Souls is different from other old colleges in Oxford, only offering places to graduates, by invitation, competition, or examination. You won't see or hear any of the usual evidence of student life, just the profound silence of scholarly thought—or it might be of absence, as many of the Fellows only attend at the weekends.

✶ ─────────

OPENING TIMES
2–4pm Monday to
Friday, free admission.

ENTRANCE
from the High Street,
just beyond St Mary's
Church and on the same
side, heading away
from Carfax.

see map **→E3**

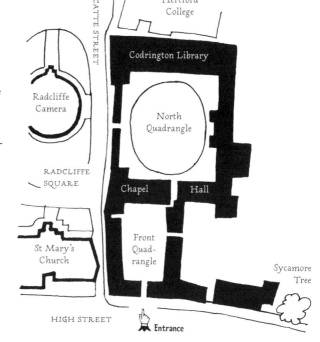

Before election
to the college
candidates were
once supposed to
have been served
cherry pie to see
what they did
with the stones.

Enter by the **Gatehouse**, noticing its carvings of Henry Chichele, Archbishop of Canterbury, and Henry VI, founders of the college in 1437, with a scene of the Resurrection.

The college was built as a memorial to honour the dead of Agincourt, where masses could be said for their souls. Before entering look along the front of the college, beyond the red telephone box, to what has been called one of the most important trees in the world; a **Sycamore tree** that plays a vital part in views along the High Street.

The **Front Quadrangle** was built first, completed in 1443, with two-storied buildings on three sides and the chapel on the fourth. A row of eight larger windows on one side mark the position of the Old Library.

The entrance to the **Chapel** is from the corner of the Quad via a porch and passageway. It is the usual college T-shape, made up of the antechapel (where you enter) and the chapel itself, divided by a Classical wooden screen, built in 1716 to replace a Medieval one. Look through the screen to the remarkable reredos that fills the east wall above the altar. It was disfigured in the Reformation, boarded over for a succession of paintings and restored in 1870, when all the figures were recarved. The antechapel has beautiful Medieval stained glass. Look out for St Jerome in his red robes and big hat, using a lion's back as a desk. The big west window is Victorian. The antechapel is crowded with monuments of the college's eminent dead, and you may discover the great feather duster of All Souls.

The **North Quadrangle** completed in 1734 is four times bigger than the Front Quad. Opposite as you enter is the **Codrington Library**, a mirror in design of the Chapel, to the right are the twin-towered Fellow's rooms and common room, to the left a cloister and gatehouse onto Radcliffe Square. The chapel side was continued in the same style for the **Hall**. All this was prompted by a bequest of £10,000 from a former Fellow, Christopher Codrington, who made his fortune in West Indian sugar. The architect was Nicholas Hawksmoor, working in a forceful reinterpretation of the gothic style of the earlier college buildings. Along the cloister hang hatchments, heraldic shields of the college Wardens.

The emblem of the college is the mallard duck which flew up from the college foundations when they were being dug. Every one hundred years on Mallard Day the Fellows process around the grounds and clamber over the roof at night, singing the mallard song, carrying a dead duck on a pole and led by Lord Mallard in a sedan chair. The next occasion isn't until 14 January 2101. Put it in your diary.

On the library is an elaborate sundial of 1658, probably designed by Christopher Wren, college bursar at the time. Its motto *Pereunt et imputator* translates as 'They pass and are reckoned', referring to the hours, or perhaps the Fellows.

Other Colleges

There are three ancient colleges along Turl Street that you could visit in one go, if you time it right and enjoy some luck.

Exeter College has a tremendously tall Victorian chapel with a tapestry by William Morris and Edward Burne-Jones, students together at Exeter, and both later associated with the Pre-Raphaelite Brotherhood of artists.
Turl Street | *map* →D3 | Open daily 2–5pm, normally

Jesus College was traditionally inhabited by Welsh students; it has two attractive small quadrangles.
Turl Street | *map* →D3 | Open daily 2–4pm, usually

Lincoln College also has two small-scale quadrangles. It took over adjoining All Saints Church in 1975 and converted it into a library. Attractive stained glass in the 17th-century chapel. Turl Street | *map* →D3 | Open Monday–Saturday 2–5pm, and Sunday 11am–5pm, maybe

there is another interesting clutch of colleges in the Broad Street vicinity

Trinity College has an outstanding chapel interior of exquisite carved wood and stucco, not to be missed.
Broad Street | *map* →D3 | Open Tuesday–Sunday 10.30am–12pm, 2–4pm; Monday in summer, possibly

Balliol College is an interesting, but unharmonious conglomeration of mostly Victorian buildings, erected at a time when Balliol was the intellectual powerhouse of the University.
Broad Street | *map* →D3 | Open 2pm–dusk with a charge for admission, sometimes

Wadham College is harmonious because it was built all in one go in the 17th century, and it has a lovely garden.
Parks Road | *map* →D2 | Open term time 1–4.30pm; outside of term time 10.30–11.45am and 1–4.30pm, customarily

Hertford College is small and has the Bridge of Sighs over New College Lane. Catte Street | *map* →E3 | Open daily 10am–dusk, probably

if you are heading down the High Street, here are three more

Queen's College has the grandest frontage on the High Street, and one of the best-looking bus-stops in the land.
High Street | *map* ➔E3 | Open only to official Oxford guided tours (alas).

University College is a contestant for the oldest college foundation, in 1249. Shelley, its most famous pupil, was expelled.
High Street | *map* ➔E3 | Not open at all, ever, so there!

St Edmund Hall is visited by diverting a little way up Queen's Lane. Halls, the forerunners of colleges, were hostels rented by Masters where students lodged and were taught.
St Edmund was the last surviving hall, until it became a college in 1957.   High Street | *map* ➔E3 | Open during daylight hours, hurrah!

south of the High Street, in the vicinity of Christ Church and Merton colleges

Oriel College Three contrasting old quadrangles. In case the college is closed you can at least get a glimpse of the remarkable hall porch and its statues from the lodge gate.
Oriel Square | *map* ➔E4 | Open 2–5pm or dusk, mostly

Corpus Christi College has an unusual pelican sundial in the quadrangle and a garden that overlooks Christ Church Meadow.   Merton Street | *map* ➔E4 | Open daily 1.30–4.30pm, as a rule

and finally here are three interesting colleges further afield

Worcester College has beautiful wooded gardens and a lake.
Beaumont Street | *map* ➔B3 | Open 2–5pm or dusk, chiefly

Keble College is a fine example of full-blown Victorian Gothic architecture in multi-coloured brick. Quite an eyeful.
Parks Road | *map* ➔D1 | Open 2–5pm or dusk, generally

St Catherine's College is an uncompromising product of the 20th century, a startling contrast to most Oxford colleges.
Manor Road | *map* ➔F2 | Open daily 2–5pm gardens only, ordinarily

At the end of this guidebook (pages 92–95) there are a series of maps to help you locate things.

1. D–K4!

When Alice found herself standing before this arched doorway, she puzzled over what to do as there was one bell-handle marked "Visitors' Bell", and another marked "Servants' Bell", but she was a Queen. Fortunately the door opened a little way, and a creature with a long beak put its head out for a moment and said "No admittance till the week after next!" and shut the door again with a bang. Hopefully you will have better luck during your visit.

The Buildings of the University

You might like to think of Oxford as a big chessboard where the city and University have been playing a game of chess for hundreds of years. It was a violent contest at first, sometimes as illogical as the chess game Alice finds herself part of when she has her adventures *Through the Looking Glass*. Now it has settled into a more gentlemanly, slow-moving affair, with no end in sight. The University seems to be getting the better of it, taking over more and more squares on the board by the unpredictable moves of its dons, the inexorable strategies of its masters, presidents, and provosts, and the sheer mass of its swarming student pawns.

As a result, Oxford is not all that it seems. What looks like a church turns out to be a library, a Victorian villa is really a department of Criminological Research, and everywhere there are the signs—milk cartons on windowsills, piles of bicycles— of student occupation.

⑧ Bodleian Library

From its humble one-room beginnings in the 14th century, the Bodleian today has become one of the great libraries of the world, in the process expanding to take under its wing a surrounding complex of ancient and beautiful buildings. As well as being the main research library of the University, it is also a copyright deposit library—and so is entitled to claim any book published in the British Isles.

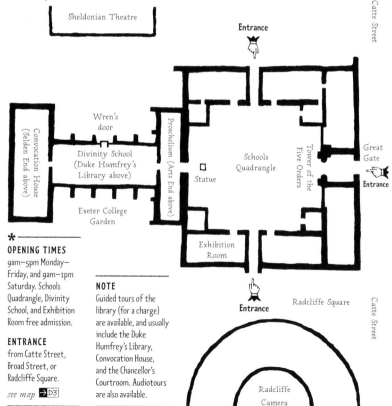

OPENING TIMES
9am–5pm Monday–Friday, and 9am–1pm Saturday. Schools Quadrangle, Divinity School, and Exhibition Room free admission.

ENTRANCE
from Catte Street, Broad Street, or Radcliffe Square.

see map ➔ D3

NOTE
Guided tours of the library (for a charge) are available, and usually include the Duke Humfrey's Library, Convocation House, and the Chancellor's Courtroom. Audiotours are also available.

The University's first library began under Bishop Cobham in the 1320s and was housed in the University Church of St Mary. In 1488 a purpose-built library room was added to the upper floor of the Divinity School, and named in honour of Duke Humfrey of Gloucester, who had donated hundreds of manuscripts to it. This was ruthlessly sacked in 1550 by Protestant reformers commissioned by King Edward VI to root out and destroy superstitious imagery. The University lacked the funds or will to restock it, sold off the furniture, and left it unused, bare, and with a leaking roof.

When Sir Thomas Bodley (1545–1613) retired to England in 1596 after a successful diplomatic career, he went to Oxford, where he had been educated, determined to refit the library at his own cost and 'stirre up other mens benevolence to help to furnish it with bookes'. The new library, soon to bear his name, was reopened in 1602 with a stock of 2,000 books. Bodley went further, ensuring a constant supply of books by negotiating an agreement with the Worshipful Company of Stationers in London; they agreed to send a free copy of every new book published, except those he rejected as 'idle bookes & riffe raffes'. He made sure of space for the books by first funding the 'Arts End' extension to Duke Humfrey's library, and then by leaving money in his will for the extension on the top floor of his library above the Schools Quadrangle, for which he also organized the necessary fund-raising.

The grand entrance to the Bodleian Library complex is through the **Great Gate** in Catte Street. It is divided into five ranges of moulded panels, studded with jewel ornament and displaying shields of the arms of the University, of James I, the Prince of Wales, and of the seventeen colleges founded by 1613, the date this building was begun.

Between 1992 and 2001 the library issued its own stamps of the value 10p, 15p, and £1 to enable payment of readers' photocopying bills. It was a Library rule that they could not be reproduced, but now that they are no longer used, we can show them here.

On the other side of the door is the impressive **Schools Quadrangle**, built between 1613 and 1620. Around the quad are doorways, once giving access to lecture rooms. The 17th-century student hoping to become a Master of Arts would be expected to study each of the subjects still inscribed in gold above the doors. At the far end are the higher schools: Medicine, Jurisprudence (Law), and through the central door Theology, the most highly esteemed of all, in the Divinity School. The top floor of the quad was used as a library extension, picture gallery, and promenade for scholars. By the 19th century however, books had taken over all the space.

The **Tower of the Five Orders** from 1613–24 stands within the quadrangle, behind the Great Door. It is the most eye-catching feature of the Schools Quadrangle, with its dramatic demonstration of the designer's knowledge of Greek and Roman architecture, becoming fashionable in England at that time. Each floor shows a different order or style of column. The lowest is the simple, sturdy, and smooth *Tuscan*; on the first floor is *Doric*, some decoration worn like socks; the second floor has *Ionic*, with the scrolly capitals; the next *Corinthian*, the richest, framing the sculpture of King James I, Fame (blowing a trumpet) to one side of him, and the University (kneeling) on the other; and the top floor is *Composite*, a hybrid of Ionic and Corinthian.

In front of the main doorway to the library and the Divinity School is a **Bronze statue** of William Herbert, third Earl of Pembroke, poet, scholar, and Chancellor of the University. He is wearing chic three-quarter armour and the Garter below his left knee (the highest order of chivalry, which was founded in 1348). When the Earl's nephew gave the statue to the University his two Oxford guests galloped off with the detachable head the same night, afraid their host might change his mind in the morning.

The five orders of Classical capitals:

Composite

Corinthian

Ionic

Doric

Tuscan

The bronze statue of William Herbert, third Earl of Pembroke in the Schools Quadrangle, by Hubert Le Sueur. The University arms on the pedestal are reputedly unique in showing a dog-eared page in the book.

Above the main doorway are the arms of Thomas Bodley, the University, and an inscription which says, in part, that 'Thomas Bodley placed this library here for you, the University of Oxford, and for the Commonwealth of the educated.'

The Divinity School featured as the Hogwarts College Infirmary in one of the Harry Potter films.

The room presently occupied by the Bodleian's shop is known as the **Proscholium**, Latin for the forecourt to the school, namely the **Divinity School**, directly ahead. This magnificent room, built by the University for the teaching and examination of Theology, was completed in 1488. The complex stone vaulted ceiling is made up of main transverse arches and a pattern of intersecting ribs, each intersection marked by a unique carved knot or boss, in all 455, showing beasts, arms, words, initials, foliage, or biblical characters. Some *bosses* are drawn down as *pendants*, like lanterns, occupied by seated figures of saints. And overhead, above all that wonderful stonework, is the original Duke Humfrey's library.

Below is one of the 'green slips' that used to be used by readers to write out their book requests at the Bodleian Library. This paper based system finished at 4pm on the 3 October 2002 for the vast majority of books. To mark this change from paper to computer, a kindly American ensured that the final book to be ordered that day, at one minute to four, was an appropriate one . . .

Today, readers use the University's computer catalogue, OLIS (Oxford Libraries Information System), which is also available online.

Green slips are occasionally still used today for manuscripts, theses, and unusual items, and come in triplicate form. The top green part of the slip is placed in the book, the middle thin white card is placed on the bookshelf, and the bottom thick white card is kept by the Librarian's Reserve Desk, after supplying the item to the usually grateful reader. Once the green slip is completed by the reader it is sped around the buildings of the library using a wonderful pneumatic air dispatch tube system. There is a dimly lit 'nerve centre' on F floor in the New Bodleian that redirects requests to the appropriate location, to enable the item to be supplied.

2 Δ 543

BOD
1. LOCATION (OLIS only)
SHELFMARK (one work only)

STRICKLAND, HUGH EDWIN
2. AUTHOR or CATALOGUE HEADING

THE DODO AND ITS KINDRED
3. SHORT TITLE

1848
5. DATE(S) OF PUBLICATION

4. VOLUME NUMBER(S) (consecutive numbers only)

9. READER'S SIGNATURE

8. READER'S TICKET NUMBER

03 1008
0C15:59
02

⑨ The Emperors

Thirteen stone heads stand guard outside the Sheldonian Theatre and four more outside the Museum of the History of Science. The originals were commissioned by Christopher Wren and carved by William Bird in 1669. Since that time there have been three generations of grim bearded heads looking down on Broad Street. There is nothing else quite like them and no one can be certain who or what they are supposed to represent.

*
ACCESS
The fronts of the Emperors can always be seen from Broad Street. The area behind them is usually locked on Saturday afternoons, Sundays, and in the evenings.

see map D3

Opposite:
A weathered Emperor from the second set, just before its replacement in the 1970s.

These pagan presences in Christian Oxford have acquired many nicknames over the years. They include the Philosophers, the Worthies, the Caesars, the Twelve Apostles (if you're not counting), but they are perhaps best known as the Emperors. The latter was popularized by Max Beerbohm in his classic novel *Zuleika Dobson*, first published in 1911. In this, great beads of perspiration are seen glistening on the Emperors' brows after they catch sight of the *femme fatale* who will wreak such havoc amongst the undergraduates and dons.

The original heads of 1669 have been replaced twice, first by the Victorians in 1868 and again in 1972–76. The Victorian set used an inferior stone that rapidly decayed so that by the middle of the 20th century this second set of heads had become little more than shapeless lumps. John Betjeman memorably likened them to 'illustrations for a medical textbook on skin diseases'.

The third set was commissioned from a local sculptor named Michael Black who went back to the original Emperors of 1669, most of which had become garden ornaments. Five heads survived in one road alone in Oxford, whilst others turned up as far afield as Herefordshire. Each new Emperor was carved from a ton or so of Clipsham stone quarried on the borders of Rutland and Lincolnshire. In attendance during the 1976 unveiling ceremony were Morris dancers, a silver band, and Medieval hornblowers, all assisted by eighty gallons of home-made beer laid on by the sculptor.

The Emperors are well worth studying in detail for variations in hair and beard styles, as well as wreaths and garments. One head has Michael Black's initials (on a shoulder), whilst another has a bird tucked between locks of hair at the back. The sculptor was adamant that his Emperors were not portraits, and that they should be enjoyed as a gallery of grotesques or as a history of beards. Perhaps he succumbed to the temptation to include an occasional likeness?

Max Beerbohm saw the condition of the Emperors as a kind of damnation; exposed to erosion by the sun, rain, wind, and frost, and remade each time they wear away, in this way they are doomed to go on paying the price of their sins for all eternity.

The third set of Emperors arriving for their installation.

⑩ Sheldonian Theatre

The apprentice work of England's greatest architect, Christopher Wren, the Sheldonian Theatre was built in 1667, not to stage plays, but the University's ceremonies. Severely Roman on the outside, its interior is a colourful delight you can enjoy by day, or during a concert at night. An easy climb leads to a spectacular view of Oxford's spires and towers from the rooftop cupola.

✽

OPENING TIMES
10am–12.30pm and 2–3.30pm in winter (in summer until 4.30pm), Monday–Saturday. Admission £1.50 adults, £1 children and concessions (charge includes cupola).

ENTRANCE
from Broad Street or Catte Street.

see map ➡D3

NOTE
A delightful way to enjoy the interior is to attend a concert (though the top gallery seating can be a bit uncomfortable).

EXTERIOR Begin by facing the building's curved front that overlooks Broad Street and is protected by the Emperors. Christopher Wren's inspiration for this building was the Theatre of Marcellus in Rome. He presented a model of his proposed design in 1663 to the Royal Society. He was just 31 years of age and Professor of Astronomy at Oxford. But there is a lack of real Roman strength and scale to his design, especially in the pinched proportions of the ground floor arcade, the blank walls between its pilasters and the apologetic little windows. This may, in fairness, have been due to financial constraints imposed by the building's patron, Gilbert Sheldon. Wren's son later wrote that his father 'was obliged to put a stop to the bolder strokes of his Pencil, and confine the Expense within the Limits of a private purse'. There is splendid carved detail above the doorway and a Latin inscription dedicating the building to King Charles II.

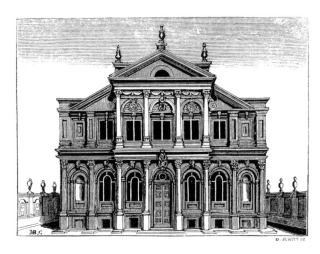

The south, more ornate, side of the Sheldonian Theatre.

Now walk around to the other side of the Sheldonian Theatre, which faces south to the Divinity School. There are doorways in both buildings which are used during the procession that is part of Encaenia, the most important ceremony in the University year, when honorary degrees are conferred. Encaenia means 'dedication' and takes place each Wednesday in the ninth week of Trinity term (towards the end of June).

The carved Latin inscription on this side of the Sheldonian dedicates the building to the University and good learning, and cites Gilbert Sheldon, Archbishop of Canterbury and Chancellor of the University, as the man who built it. (He stumped up the £14,470 11s 11d that it cost.) Sheldon's coat of arms, framed by angels and a mitre, is over the door.

The Theatre as built took on a slightly stark character, which Sir John Summerson likened to a 'very magnificent old gasometer'. The impression would have been more animated by the quirky original **roof-line** of oval dormer windows, each one wearing a gilded bishop's mitre, except for the window closest to Broad Street which had a crown. These features were done away with in 1802 during a restoration of the roof, which is a great shame as they were a delightful part of Wren's design. His cupola was replaced in 1838 by one of greater scale and presence, the work of Edward Blore.

The doorway that Wren introduced into the side of the Divinity School is framed by a sinuous gothic arch (known as an ogee) of unfurling leaves. The monogram CWA in the gable is presumably Christopher Wren, Architect. Atop the doorway is a carved book with a quote from Luke's gospel in Greek 'They found him sitting in the midst of Doctors'.

INTERIOR Enter by the side door on the east side; you will need to buy a ticket. After the severity of the exterior, all is festive and colourful, revelling in the illusions of a ceiling painted to look like the sky and wooden columns painted to look as if they are made of marble. The colours are believed to be faithful to the original scheme.

Ceremonies take place in the body of the hall, the audience seated on the tiered benches, amongst them the Chancellor on his throne, a small seat beside him reserved for Terrae Filius (son of the soil), the University Fool. From Medieval times until he was suppressed in 1713, this character was allowed to punctuate the ceremonies with satirical speeches which sometimes went too far. At the Theatre's inaugural ceremony in 1669 John Evelyn was appalled by a 'tedious, abusive, sarcastical rhapsody' from Terrae Filius. It was the offence caused by such scenes, when the ceremonies were still being held at St Mary's Church, that led directly to the building of the Sheldonian Theatre. Speeches are made from the Proctors' Rostra (a wooden pulpit), boxes decorated with gilded lions' heads. High spirits did linger on after Terrae Filius into the Victorian age. Popular sing-along songs such as 'Daddy wouldn't buy me a bow-wow' were heard as a prelude to Encaenia. At the entry of the dishevelled, long-haired Lord Tennyson to receive his honorary doctorate, he was greeted by a cry from the gallery: 'Did your mother call

The object jutting out from the lion's mouth on the Proctors' Rostra is a bundle of elm twigs bound around an axe, known as a *fasces*. It was a symbol of Roman authority, and was later used by the Fascists in Italy.

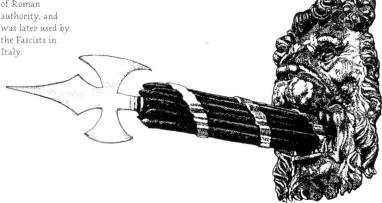

One of Wren's seventy-foot wooden roof trusses, made from scarfed-together lengths of timber, originally used in the Theatre.

you early, dear?' And when the Duke of Wellington was installed as Chancellor, there were tumultuous cheers and good-hearted amusement at his blunders in Latin.

The **ceiling**, by James Thornhill, has allegorical figures of Religion, Arts, and Science reclining on their cloud couches around the tiny central figure of Truth. Geography has a globe, Poetry a harp, and Optick peers through her telescope. Envy, a naked figure with snakes for hair is sent plummeting. The ceiling's span, seventy by eighty feet, with no supporting columns to spoil the view, was a great achievement for its time, made possible by Wren's clever design of attic roof trusses.

The theatre has had three **organs**; the current case was installed in 1877. The second organ was played by Handel for the first performance of his oratorio *Athalia* in 1733, and in 1791 Haydn directed the first performance of his symphony number 92, 'The Oxford'.

Follow directions for the rooftop cupola.

As you climb the stairs think of the University Press, who moved into the building when it opened. The printing presses were in the cellars, paper and books were stored in the attic and corridors, while compositors set up type in rooms off the landings. Work soon overflowed into the hall, but had to be packed up whenever there was a ceremony.

The **Attic** is dark following the removal of dormer windows in the last century. The timberwork of the roof is a replacement of the last century after concern over the floor, which had carried the weight of unsold Press books.

The **Cupola** was replaced in 1838 by a larger version than Wren's original, allowing more space for visitors to enjoy the panoramic view.

The building is Oxford's principal concert hall and has been able to stage evening concerts safely here since the University agreed to install electricity in 1934 after holding out against it for fifty years.

⑪ St Mary's Church

*A*s well as being a magnificent parish church, St Mary's
was adopted by the University as its first home. It served
as a place for lectures, examinations, the award of degrees,
and for a time as the vice-chancellor's court room. It was also
the scene of the dramatic preliminaries to the martyrdom
of Archbishop Cranmer, and Bishops Latimer and Ridley. Today
you can exert yourself by climbing the 127 spiralling steps
to the fine view from the tower and afterwards take a well
earned rest in the coffee house.

OPENING TIMES
9am–5pm every day,
and until 7pm during
July and August, free
admission.

Excellent views can be
had from the tower
(although perhaps not
for those prone to
vertigo) admission
£1.50 adults,
75p concessions.

ENTRANCE
from the High Street
or Radcliffe Square.
The Vaults and Garden
Café is in the
Congregation House.

see map → E3

The **Tower** and **Spire** are surely one of the finest in the country, making a spectacular contribution to the Oxford skyline. They were built in the Decorated Gothic style in the 13th and 14th centuries, more than a hundred years earlier than the main body of the church which is in the Perpendicular Gothic style. It is the sequence of gabled pinnacles extending telescopically upwards that generates all the excitment.

The infant University adopted St Mary's as its own church and in the early 14th century built the attached **Congregation House** (left of the Radcliffe Square entrance) as its first building. It was originally the meeting place for Congregation (legislative body of the University), and since has served as fire station, lecture hall, powder magazine, parish hall, book store, tyre depository, brass rubbing centre, and now a very popular coffee house and restaurant.

The **South Porch** on the High Street is the theatrical entrance, dating from 1637. Extraordinary details such as the barley sugar columns jostle to catch the eye. The contorted old **Almond tree** on its crutch makes a fine partner for the porch, especially in its springtime blossom.

The **Chancel** has an impressive height, emphasized by the relative narrowness of the space, and the natural light flooding in from above. The scarred stalls in the **Choir** date from the rebuilding of the chancel in 1463. Also Medieval is the **Reredos** (the ornamental screen behind the altar). Its seven niches are 15th-century, but the statues in them are Victorian replacements. The one on the second left is St Frideswide, a Saxon princess who is the patron saint of the City and University (see page 23).

The **Nave** was built in the 15th century. The screen, pulpit, font, pews, gallery, and internal porches mostly date from the 19th century. The effect is rather chilling, and not helped by the black and white paving of 1673. The Victorian **West Window** is by C. E. Kempe, with its theme of the Tree of Jesse. The **Organ** was built in 1987 by Metzler Orgelbau of Zurich, in a traditional style that still looks terrifically new. Above the gallery is a roof boss showing Mahatma Gandhi, who spent a weekend in Oxford in 1931.

Graffiti recently festooned the room in which the church bells are rung in the tower. I would be interested to know their translation, but please don't add your own.

The **Adam de Brome Chapel** is named after the rector of the church and the founder of Oriel College. One of the pillars of the nave closest to the Brome chapel has a chunk knocked out of it near its base. This was supposedly where a corner of a temporary stage was fixed in 1556 for the trial of Archbishop Cranmer and so is known as **Cranmer's Pillar**.

From the **Pulpit** of 1827 congregations packed the church to hear John Henry Newman, vicar of St Mary's Church 1828–1843, and the other leaders of the Oxford Movement.

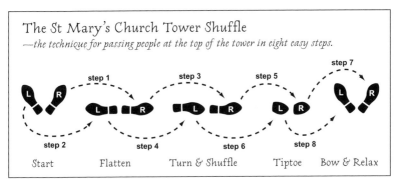

The St Mary's Church Tower Shuffle
—the technique for passing people at the top of the tower in eight easy steps.

Start — Flatten — Turn & Shuffle — Tiptoe — Bow & Relax

⑫ Botanic Garden

Its purpose is the same as it was when it was founded in 1621: 'to promote learning and glorify the works of God'. It has grown into one of the most diverse collections of plants in the world, with over 6,500 species within its four and a half acres. There is more diversity here than in a tropical rain forest. Contribute to that diversity by taking yourself on an enlightening stroll around.

✱

OPENING TIMES
April–September
9am–5pm (glasshouses
10am–4.30pm,
usually), and
October–March
9am–4.30pm
(glasshouses
10am–4pm).
Admission charge in
summer only.
www.botanic-garden.
ox.ac.uk

ENTRANCE
from the High
Street.

see map ➔ F4

NOTE
Some plants in the
garden are toxic so
don't pick or eat them.

Most visitors approach from the High Street and their first sight is of the modern garden of roses and clipped hedges commemorating Oxford's wartime contribution to the development of penicillin. Then you are confronted by the tremendously grand **Danby Arch**, a stone gateway built in 1633 and designed by Nicholas Stone, Inigo Jones's master mason. Lord Danby, who gave £5000 to set up the garden, was inspired by such gardens in Italy and Holland when he and his brother were on the run after the murder of their neighbour in a family feud. They were later pardoned by Queen Elizabeth I. That's Lord Danby's bust in the topmost pediment. The full-length figures are Charles I and Charles II.

Go through the entrance next to the arch. The garden you see enclosed within its walls was built at the same time as the arch, and is the oldest such garden in the United Kingdom. It's a formal layout of oblong beds displaying plants grouped in their botanical families, to assist in the garden's primary purpose of providing material for the teaching of botany within the University. All the plants are labelled. You may even come across the 'Economic beds', for plants that have been important to man, including the humble potato, *Solanum tuberosum*.

Beyond the walls, straight ahead, where the garden was extended after the Second World War, are different areas, including a walk beside the River Cherwell, a rock garden, an herbaceous border, and a bog garden. On the river side beyond the wall to your left are the glasshouses. In the **Tropical House** are water lilies, papyrus, and banana. The President of the Royal College of Physicians is entitled to half the annual banana crop; the other half goes to the President of Magdalen College. The **Palm House** has citrus fruits, coffee, cocoa, coconut, as well as palms. The **Succulent House** has plants from arid parts of the world, carnivorous plants and *Agave ferox*, the century plant, which spectacularly bloomed for the first time in 1995 after living in the house since 1874, then expired. There is also a **Fernery**, and an **Alpine House**.

There are some 150 different trees growing in the garden. The oldest is the yew by the lily pond, planted in 1650 by the garden's first Superintendent, or *Horti Praefectus*, Jacob Bobart, who tagged his beard with silver on high days and holidays, and was followed everywhere by his pet goat. A hybrid plane tree grown by Bobart's son Jacob the Younger, the next Superintendent, was the origin of the pollution-resistant London Plane which became such a feature of Britain's city streets. The huge surviving tree at Magdalen College (see page 26) is a direct descendant.

The most successful escapee from the garden is the weed *Senecio squalidus*. Sown from seeds sent from Mount Etna, it scaled the walls and, once it reached the railway, spread rapidly in the wake of trains. The cindered railway cuttings provided similar conditions to the volcanic terrain of its country of origin. The weed became known as Oxford ragwort.

You may notice what look like lengths of pipe stuck to the wall on the east side of the garden. These are artifical nests designed to attract female mason bees, potential pollinators for the plants.

The imposing Danby Gate, the formal entrance to the Botanic Garden, guarded by a skulking don.

Other buildings of the University

Please note there is usually no public access to the buildings
listed below, we include them here for their prominent exteriors.

⁑ Clarendon Building

corner of Broad Street and Catte Street | *see map* ➔D3
No public access, except for the central passageway and steps

The Clarendon Building is one of the most impressive of
the buildings that dominate the eastern end of Broad
Street. It was built in 1713 for Oxford University Press,
who moved here from their first home next door in the
Sheldonian Theatre. The building was named after the
first Earl of Clarendon, who gave the Press the copyright
of his best-selling *The History of the Great Rebellion*. His
statue, in the robes of Lord Chancellor of England, is on
the side of the building, looking down Broad Street. The
Press later moved, and the Clarendon Building is now part
of the Bodleian Library. The architect, Nicholas
Hawksmoor, worked at first as an assistant to Christopher
Wren and later with John Vanburgh on Blenheim Palace.
The only public access is to the central passageway and the
steps to Broad Street are a favourite perch for exhausted
visitors and lunchtime workers. On the roof are nine statues of the Muses, seven in lead and two replacements in
fibreglass unveiled in 1974 by two brave ladies in flimsy
Grecian robes to a fanfare by Bugle Major Len Bucknell.

⁑ Radcliffe Camera

Radcliffe Square | *see map* ➔D3
No public access

The Radcliffe Camera is the magnificent domed building
that you can't miss in the centre of Radcliffe Square. It
was built between 1736 and 1749 as an independent
medical and scientific library with money left by the fashionable physician John Radcliffe. His trustees spent over

twenty years buying up land to create the square and appointed James Gibbs as architect. In 1862 the Bodleian Library took over the building as reading rooms, renaming it the Radcliffe Camera. A two storey underground book store lies beneath the grass and cobbles of the square, connected to the Bodleian Library by tunnel and beyond that to the New Bodleian via a conveyor belt under Broad Street.

⁂ New Bodleian Library

Broad Street | *see map* ➜D2
No public access

The New Bodleian Library by Giles Gilbert Scott, bulks large on Broad Street opposite the Clarendon Building, housing millions of books, but winning no prizes for its looks. At the New Bodleian's official opening by George VI in 1946 the ceremonial silver key broke in the lock.

⁂ Indian Institute

Broad Street, at Catte Street end | *see map* ➜D2
No public access

The Indian Institute was built in 1883 to the design of Basil Champneys to encourage the study of India by the west and vice versa, and is now the History Faculty branch of the Bodleian Library. There are carvings of Hindu gods and animals, a gilded elephant weathervane, and a brass plaque in Sanskrit in the porch.

⁂ Examination Schools

High Street | *see map* ➜E3
No public access

The Examination Schools building looks like a Jacobean country house that has strayed. It was designed by T. G. Jackson (see Brasenose and Hertford colleges) and built 1876–82, severely stretching the University's finances. Notice the sculpted panels over the main entrance, showing a viva voce examination and the MA degree ceremony.

Now you've reached the real heart of this guidebook, the bit where you can find out about me and my tragic remains on display at the Oxford University Museum of Natural History. It's no good feeling squeamish—you will have to go past a lot of other dead things before you find me.

This scene from Lewis Carroll's *Alice's Adventures in Wonderland* shows a party of animals after their swim in a pool of tears. They are trying to get dry by listening to the mouse recite the driest thing it knows, an extract from a history text book that begins 'William the Conqueror, whose cause was furthered by the Pope ...'. You will find inanimate versions of many of these creatures on display on the upper floor of the Museum. In the book they are disguises for friends and acquaintances of Lewis Carroll, who thought of himself as the Dodo.

Museums in Oxford

Oxford's annual influx of new students helps to stop the city from becoming one big museum, a repository of curious old buildings and even more curious traditions. For most visitors the colleges and University buildings are the main thing to see, but please don't ignore the museums. Over the next few pages we have highlighted a couple of world-class ones, and provided shorter accounts of the best of the rest.

Here we see the Mad Hatter from *Alice's Adventures in Wonderland*. He seems to be suggesting some additions to the Pitt Rivers Museum. Incidentally, felt hat makers were frequently sent mad by the effects of mercury poisoning in the manufacturing process; but this wasn't realized for many years.

⑬ Ashmolean Museum and Cast Gallery

The Ashmolean has probably the best collection of art and antiquities in the country, outside of London, and certainly doesn't deserve to be kept just for a rainy day. There must be something to tempt you, whether it's a drawing by Michelangelo, a Stradivarius violin, or the deerskin mantle of Powhatan, the father of Pocahontas.

ASHMOLEAN MUSEUM

✱ ———————
OPENING TIMES
10am–5pm Tuesday–
Saturday, and 12–5pm
Sunday. Free admission.
Note: the museum will
remain open during a
major redevelopment
of the site starting in
2006, but some
galleries will be closed.
01865 278000
www.ashmol.ox.ac.uk

ENTRANCE
from Beaumont
Street.

see map ➡ C2
———————

A four
thousand
year old
Cycladic
figure
from the
islands
between
Greece and
Turkey.

ASHMOLEAN MUSEUM

The Ashmolean is the oldest public museum in Britain, opened on 21 May 1683. Its origins lie in the cabinet of curiosities collected by John Tradescant, Keeper of His Majesty's Gardens, Vines, and Silkworms and added to by his son, also named John, who opened it to the public at six-pence each. Elias Ashmole, a lawyer fascinated by all that was ancient and curious, paid for a catalogue to be printed, eventually inheriting the collection from the family and persuading the University of Oxford to house it in the building in Broad Street now known as The Museum of the History of Science (see page 70). Parts of that collection were moved, with the University's collection of art, to this building in Beaumont Street, under the name of The Ashmolean Museum, in 1894. You can see portraits of Ashmole and the Tradescants in room 38 at the top of the stairs on the first floor. Next door in room 27 are some surviving exhibits from the original collection, including Powhatan's Mantle, and Guy Fawkes's lantern, which he was supposed to be carrying when he was about to blow up Parliament. There's also a hat fortified with iron worn by one of the judges who pronounced the death sentence on King Charles I and clearly feared for his own safety.

The Museum exhibits are far too various to attempt to describe so we'll select a few favourites. It's advisable to get yourself a plan from the shop as it's easy to get lost.

GROUND FLOOR Room 13 has a collection of **Chinese paintings** cleverly displayed in a new space so that you can view the tall scroll paintings from a raised gallery as well as close to. There are ravishingly beautiful **Japanese painted folding screens** in room 19. Also on this floor is the Museum shop.

FIRST FLOOR In room 39 are Italian Renaissance paintings. Always popular is Uccello's **The Hunt in the Forest**, a tapestry-like pattern of hurrying huntsmen, hounds, and deer in a mysterious dark forest, that is also an instructive exercise in perspective. Nearby on the same wall is the even more mysterious **Forest Fire** by Piero di Cosimo, full of exotic beasts and birds (no dodos in sight, but look out for a pig and a deer with human heads). In room 30, devoted to antiquities from the Aegean, you will find some strangely modern-looking **Cycladic figurines**, reminiscent of 20th-century sculpture. Their function is unknown. Room 35 has a very precious Anglo-Saxon object, **King Alfred's jewel**. The Ashmolean's recently opened room the **Sands Gallery** (47) is also on this floor, a fascinating collection of **20th-century British art**.

SECOND FLOOR Room 56 has some fine Pre-Raphaelite paintings by Holman Hunt and John Millais.

LOWER GROUND FLOOR Has a lecture theatre, café, and toilets.

CAST GALLERY

Round the corner, via St John Street, is hidden away the **Cast Gallery** in Pusey Place (still part of the Ashmolean Museum), where you can mingle with an impressive crowd of plaster casts of Greek and Roman sculptures.

King Alfred's jewel, made by Anglo–Saxon craftsmen in the 9th century (room 35 on the first floor). It's made of gold, enamel, and rock crystal, with an inscription AELFRED MEC HEHYT GEWYRCAN that translates as 'Alfred ordered me to be made'. The figure portrayed has one black eye and one grey and probably isn't the king.

CAST GALLERY

* —————————
OPENING TIMES
10am–4pm
Tuesday– Friday, and
10am–1pm Saturday.
Free admission.
01865 278079

ENTRANCE
from Pusey Place.
see map ➜C2

⑭ University Museum of Natural History and Pitt Rivers Museum

A unique experience, perhaps even more enjoyable for its architecture and decoration than its contents, and of course a place of pilgrimage for all Dodo enthusiasts. A great bonus is the presence of a second museum —the extraordinary gallimaufry of the Pitt Rivers.

UNIVERSITY MUSEUM

*
OPENING TIMES
12–5pm every day
except Easter and
Christmas closures.
Free admission.
01865 272949
www.oum.ox.ac.uk

ENTRANCE
from Parks Road.
see map ➔D1

If it's summer, watch for swifts going in and out of the ventilator flues in the top of the tower. Their nest sites have been studied by scientists since 1948, and can often be watched on close-circuit television images from inside the museum.

THE UNIVERSITY MUSEUM OF NATURAL HISTORY

As you approach the museum, perhaps even across the grass (yes, you can do that here) and cross the tracks of the megalosaurus, notice that the building is in a Medieval style. This was unusual for museums in the 1850s; serious buildings were usually Classical. The designers even seem to be making a joke by separating off the chemical laboratory (the chapel-like building with pointed roof and big chimneys) as a copy of the Abbot's Kitchen at Glastonbury, presumably because both buildings had to deal with smells. Before entering the porch look at the carving around the nearby windows, much of it incomplete. The carving on the arch over the outer door is also unfinished; legend has it that the red bearded O'Shea brothers, talented stonemasons from Ireland, got into trouble and were dismissed for making parrots and owls as parodies of University dons. A more probable reason was a lack of funds which led to the failure to complete the carvings. On entering the porch notice the delightful metalwork of the door handles and hinges.

The interior is a surprise: a forest of slender cast iron columns supporting a glass roof, materials until then usually associated with railway stations. The quality of detail continues here, the columns sprouting fantastic wrought iron leaves, and the supporting struts and ribs shaped and perforated in Medieval patterns. It's as if we are inside the body of some great creature as we look up through the ribs of Tyranosaurus rex to the arched ribs and scales of the glazed roof. Around the central court are arcades of columns, each one of a different polished stone identified by painted lettering on its plinth. The capitals are brilliantly carved with plant forms based on specimens brought to the O'Sheas from the Botanic Garden. Statues of famous scientists (and Prince Albert) lean down to inspire us. Don't fail to go to the upper floor for more exhibits, live insects, and great views of the architecture. Use the stairs by the lift and you will see the working beehive.

Pride of place in the collection must of course go to the precious relics of our guide the Oxford Dodo. It's just a mummified head and foot, but there's a handsome reconstruction in a display case that tells the whole sorry story. The next door case celebrates the work of Charles Dodgson, better known as Lewis Carroll, the author of *Alice's Adventures in Wonderland*.

Here I am with my old friend Mr Charles Darwin. I remember explaining to him that once I'd had wings and could fly. He gave me a look of disbelief, but I could see I'd given him something to think about ...

Incidently, you can buy excellent portraits of me at the book and gift shop in the Museum.

THE PITT RIVERS MUSEUM

This is entered from the far end of the ground floor of the University Museum. After the light under the glass roof of the Museum, the Pitt Rivers is like a dark attic crammed from floor to ceiling with so many things that you just don't know where to start. It is a place devoted to the study of mankind and its cultures based on the original collection given to the University by Lieutenant-General Augustus Henry Lane Fox Pitt Rivers in 1883. More has been acquired since, from forty foot totem poles carved from the trunk of a single tree, to shrunken heads. You might stumble upon anything, even the stoppered bottle supposed to contain a witch. There is also an offshoot of the Museum at 60 Banbury Road called the **Balfour Building**, which is a research and study centre for musical instruments, textiles and clothing, and is open to the public by appointment only (telephone 01865 270927).

PITT RIVERS MUSEUM

✱———————

OPENING TIMES
12–4.30pm Monday–Saturday, and 2–4.30pm Sunday. Free admission.
01865 270927
www.prm.ox.ac.uk

ENTRANCE
from within the University Museum of Natural History, Parks Road.

see map ➜D1

Other Museums

※ Museum of the History of Science

Broad Street | *see map* →D3
Open 12–4pm Tuesday–Saturday, 2–5pm Sunday, closed Bank Holidays and Christmas week, free admission, visitors' shop. Telephone 01865 277280, Website www.mhs.ox.ac.uk

Where museums began, this was the first museum building in the country to open to the public, in 1683. It was also the first building specifically designed for the study of science and holds what may be the world's finest collection of early astronomical, mathematical, and optical instruments. These are things of beauty as well as historic interest. As a result of recent renovation work, there is a fascinating display of things found on the site, such as skeletal material from dissections and chemical vessels from the original laboratory. It is a fine building in its own right, housing the original Ashmolean collection before it was moved in the 19th century to a purpose-built grander building in Beaumont Street (see page 66 for more information).

※ Modern Art Oxford

30 Pembroke Street | *see map* →C4
Open 11am–5.30m Tuesday–Wednesday and Friday–Saturday, 11am–8pm Thursday, and 12–5.30pm Sunday. Telephone for Public Holiday times. Admission charge, visitors' shop, and a good café. Telephone 01865 722733, Website www.modernartoxford.org.uk

Temporary exhibitions of challenging contemporary art, plus a programme of talks, special events, and live music.

※ Museum of Oxford

Blue Boar Street (off St Aldates) | *see map* →D4
Open 10am–4pm Tuesday–Saturday, 12–4pm Sunday, admission charge, visitors' shop, audio tour. Telephone 01865 252761, Website www.aliceinoxford.net

The history of the city and its people, including recreations of an Elizabethan Inn, an 18th-century college room, a

Victorian kitchen, a 1930s living room, and Lewis Carroll and Alice. There are also temporary exhibitions about local authors, artists, and aspects of the bygone social scene.

✳ The Oxford Story

6 Broad Street | *see map* ➡D3
Open January–June and September–December: 10am–4.30pm Monday–Saturday, 11am–4.30pm Sunday, otherwise July–August: 9.30am–5pm; closed Christmas Day, admission charge, gift shop, audio guides in different languages. Telephone 01865 728822. Website www.oxfordstory.co.uk

Not really a museum but a different way of learning about the history of the University, in the form of a seated ride through historic scenes, complete with sounds and smells. An interactive exhibition lets you use touch screens to interrogate experts from the University.

✳ Bate Collection of Musical Instruments

St Aldates | *see map* ➡D5
Open 2–5pm Monday–Friday, and 10am–12pm Saturday (during full term only), free admission, visitors' shop. Telephone 01865 276139. Website www.ashmol.ox.ac.uk/BCMIPage.html

If you are interested in musical instruments there is an embarrassment of riches in Oxford. This collection alone has over a thousand historic instruments on permanent display. There is also the **Pitt Rivers Museum** on Parks Road and its outpost called the **Balfour Building** at 60 Banbury Road (see page 69).

✳ Oxford University Press Museum

Great Clarendon Street | *see map* ➡B1
Open by prior appointment only, office hours, Monday–Friday, free admission. Telephone 01865 353527

Oxford University Press has a small museum devoted to the history of its printing and publishing since the 15th century, and includes various books, documents, and printing equipment.

Here we see the Dodo, Alice, and their friends at the conclusion of the Caucus-race in *Alice's Adventures in Wonderland*. The rules of the Caucus-race seem to be that the contestants begin running around a racecourse, of no particular shape, whenever they like, and stop whenever they like. Everybody wins and everybody gets prizes. The Dodo is presenting Alice with her prize, a thimble she had been forced to donate herself. In case you don't know, a Caucus is a system of organization by committees.

Other things to do

When you have had your fill of the main sights of Oxford you may find there is still the time or inclination to do something else, something un-touristy. It may not be as strenuous as taking part in a Caucus-race (see opposite), but it might be punting, walking, cycling, reading, or lazing about in an interesting place. We hope the next few pages will provide some inspiration.

Of course there is always shopping.

The main shopping streets are Cornmarket and Queen Street (linked by the Clarendon Centre arcade), the Westgate Centre at the end of Queen Street, the High Street, Broad Street, Magdalen Street, and not forgetting the delights of the Covered Market. More specialised shops can be found in Little Clarendon Street, which is off the Woodstock Road at the far end of St Giles.

Punting

*Poling idly along the waters of the Cherwell or Isis
in a punt is so much a part of everyone's idea of
Oxford that you may feel keen to have a go yourself.
Drift into the sun-dappled idyll of an Edwardian
golden age. Don't forget your straw boater!*

WHAT IS A PUNT? It's a square-ended, flat-bottomed craft
manoeuvred with a pole, native to the River Thames and
once used for ferrying, fishing, and light transport. Now it
is entirely used for recreation, especially at Oxford and
Cambridge, where shallow waters undisturbed by the wash
of power boats allow their survival.

Please remember to
let go of the pole if
it gets stuck in the
mud on the river
bottom, otherwise
you might be left
hanging from the
pole while the punt
glides serenely down
the river.

WHERE TO DO IT There are three hiring places. The most central is at Howard's Landing Stage on the River Cherwell
(pronounced char-wel), down the slope beside **Magdalen Bridge**
(pronounced mawd-lin in Oxford, but mag-duh-lin in Cambridge) on the college side (map ➡F4, telephone 01865
202643). On the same river is the **Cherwell Boathouse**,
approached along Bardwell Road off the Banbury Road in
north Oxford (telephone 01865 515978) where punt building still goes on and there is a restaurant too. The Cherwell
between these two hiring places is beautiful, passing the
University Parks, the island called Mesopotamia (Greek for
between two rivers), Parsons' Pleasure (the traditional place
for nude male bathing), and the Rollers where punts are
pushed up or rolled down a change of level at a weir. Above
the Cherwell Boathouse, the Victoria Arms is an isolated
riverside pub where refreshment may be sought. The third
hiring place is at **Folly Bridge** on the Isis, approached by
St Aldates (map ➡D5, telephone 0961 115369).

WHEN TO DO IT During term time it can be difficult to hire
punts because of block bookings by colleges. July and August

should be easier and September quiet and beautiful if the weather is kind.

DO IT IN STYLE by buying the ingredients for a picnic in the Covered Market (*see* page 80).

DON'T DO IT And for those unsure about the whole thing you could always treat it as a spectator sport, or get an easier taste of life on the river by taking one of the scheduled **boat trips** from Folly Bridge run by Salter Brothers (map ➜D5], telephone 01865 243421).

As you are in Oxford, you should stand at the sloping end of the punt (see illustration to point 1 below), instead of following the Cambridge tradition of punting from the square end.

HOW TO PUNT

The forward foot should remain in the same position throughout. If this is your first time punting then practice lifting and balancing the pole whilst you are still on dry land. At the end of each stroke, before removing the pole from the water, you should use it to steer the punt.

1 Stand at the rear, sloping end, of the punt. The forward hand brings the pole and body weight towards the front of the punt.

2 Rear hand throws the pole forward, whilst the forward hand catches it at the point of balance.

3 Both hands raise the pole.

4 Drop the pole into the water, with the hands controlling its placement. The pole is not quite vertical.

5 Rear hand reaches up to grip the pole, as the bottom of the pole touches the river bottom.

6 Forward hand grips the pole just above the rear hand, and together they push the punt forward.

7 Hands and body move back as the body turns to the side and the pole is lifted. Use the pole just before it leaves the water to steer the punt, by pushing to the left to steer to the left, and vice versa.

Disclaimer
The authors cannot be held responsible for the accuracy of these guidelines; indeed we suggest the use of a complete punt, rather than the partial punt shown here.

Literature, Theatre, and Cinema

Even in our technological age Oxford is still a city made as much of paper as it is of brick and stone. Many of the great names of English Literature have passed along its streets, dreaming of success, or revisited them in imagination.

LITERATURE

Queen Victoria much admired *Alice* and wrote to Dodgson for anything else he'd written. He sent her his *Syllabus of Plane Algebraical Geometry*, an altogether more academic book.

We must be selective, and as so much of Oxford strikes people as fantastic nonsense, here are some specialists in that genre. **Charles Lutwidge Dodgson** (1832-98) spent most of his life at Christ Church as student, lecturer in Mathematics, shy bachelor don, and ordained Deacon, with a fondness for photography and storytelling. On a trip up the river to God-stow on 4 July 1862 with Alice Liddell, daughter of the Dean, he told his usual stories, but afterwards published them, as *Alice's Adventures in Wonderland*, under the *nom de plume* of **Lewis Carroll**. The shop where Alice bought her favourite barley sugar is still opposite Christ Church.

Another much-loved fantasy for children of all ages is *Wind in the Willows* by **Kenneth Grahame** (1859-1932), featuring a Mole, a Rat, and a Toad, but no Dodo. Grahame was at school in Oxford, bequeathed the copyright income from his book to the Bodleian Library, and was buried at Holywell Cemetery. The classic Edwardian satiric fantasy *Zuleika Dobson* by **Max Beerbohm** (1872-1956) chronicles the visit of a heroine so beautiful that the student population commit suicide. Still on our theme, **J. R. R. Tolkein** (1892-1973) was Professor of Anglo-Saxon, but is better known for *The Lord of the Rings*. His friend **C. S. Lewis** (1898-1963) was a Fellow at Magdalen, but similarly created memorable fantasy worlds in books such as *The Lion, The Witch and The Wardrobe*.

Oxford has continued to inspire fantasy. Local author **Philip Pullman**'s trilogy *His Dark Materials*, featuring the twelve year old heroine Lyra, begins in Oxford, at fictional Jordan College. The tremendously popular *Harry Potter* stories, by **J. K. Rowling** tell of a schoolboy who becomes a wizard. For the film versions Christ Church was one of the venues used for Hogwarts School of Witchcraft and Wizardry. A surprising success of 2003 was *The Curious Incident of the Dog in the Night-Time* by another local author, **Mark Haddon**. Detection in Oxford is in the safe hands of *Inspector Morse* in the stories by **Colin Dexter** which were made into a popular TV series. Also fondly remembered on TV is the serialization of **Evelyn Waugh's** *Brideshead Revisited*, the classic account of dissipated student life in 1920s Oxford.

If you want to buy books then you are spoilt for choice. **Blackwell's**, Broad Street, was founded in 1879 and the main shop (opposite the Sheldonian Theatre) also includes secondhand books and a café. Blackwell's has other shops in Broad Street—next door to the main shop is one specializing in books about Oxford and by Oxford authors. There is also **Waterstones** on the corner of Broad Street and Cornmarket, **Borders** in Magdalen Street, and **W. H. Smith** in Cornmarket. For secondhand books try **Waterfields** in the High Street, and the **Oxfam Bookshop** in St Giles.

THEATRE AND CINEMA

Shakespeare's company often performed in Oxford and drama keeps a lively presence today. The **Playhouse** in Beaumont Street is the main theatre for touring and Oxford University Dramatic Society productions, with its adjoining, smaller, **Burton Taylor Theatre** in Gloucester Street (telephone 305305). The **Pegasus Theatre**, Magdalen Street, East Oxford is a youth theatre and arts centre (telephone 722851), and the **New Theatre** in George Street is a big venue hosting opera, dance, drama, and musical companies, as well as comedy and groups (telephone 0870 606 3500). In summer term watch out for students in costume, advertising **Shakespeare** productions in the college gardens or city parks— a wonderful way to spend a balmy evening.

Oxford's central cinemas are the Odeons, in Magdalen Street and George Street (telephone 0870 505 0007), and the Phoenix in Walton Street (telephone 512526).

Tolkein and Lewis were members of an informal group calling itself *The Inklings*, that often met at the pub in St Giles called The Eagle and Child.

The **Oxford Literary Festival** is a growing feature of the city year, and usually takes place in the last week of March. Tickets and information at the Oxford Playhouse or from the festival box office at the Oxford Union.

Commemorated by a pub of the same name in Walton Street is **Thomas Hardy's** novel *Jude the Obscure*. The tragic hero, a stonemason yearning for scholarship, died embittered in the university city of Christminster (a thinly disguised Oxford).

Green Oxford

Need a break from ancient buildings? Want to rest your eyes on trees and grass, lie down with a good book, or stretch your legs on a walk? Don't worry: there's greenery throughout and around the city, from wide open spaces of meadowland to intimate examples of the garden arts.

The **University Parks** are where the Royalist army exercised its troops during the Civil War. Plenty of open space to picnic or throw your boomerang, many magnificent trees, and the University cricket ground with its handsome pavilion. On the eastern side of the park is the River Cherwell, where the graceful arch of the Rainbow Bridge leads you over to the village of Marston. Alternatively, you could follow the riverside walk south from the Parks' south-eastern corner to 'Mesopotamia'—the overgrown woodland alongside the River Cherwell. Free entry to the Parks is from Parks Road (map ➡D1], just beyond the University Museum).

Christ Church Meadow comes right up to the heart of the city and the college of Christ Church on its southern side, and is still grazed by cattle. You can walk all round its edge, start-ing either from the War Memorial Garden off St Aldate's (map ➡D4]) or from Rose Lane off the High Street (map ➡F4]). Deadman's Walk, once the way to the Jewish burial ground on what is now the Botanic Garden, passes under the city walls of Merton College on the Meadow's northern side, the Broad Walk crosses east to west, and the tree-lined Poplar Walk, planted by Dean Liddell (the father of Alice of *Alice's Adventures in Wonderland*) in 1872, runs from Christ Church south to the River Thames.

The **Botanic Garden** has one of the most diverse collections of plants in the world; pages 60–61 have a detailed description.

Port Meadow on the north-west side of the city, is over 300 acres of ancient meadow that has never been ploughed, and where freemen and commoners have had the rights to graze their cattle and horses for over a thousand years. You can reach it by going north from the city centre along Walton Street (map →B1), then turning left along Walton Well Road. A path across the meadow leads to the Perch pub at Binsey, after crossing the River Thames on a Victorian footbridge (3 kilometres or 1.5 miles). Another path, to the right, leads north to the Trout pub at Wolvercote (3 kilometres or 2 miles).

CHRIST CHURCH MEADOW.

The Meadow Keepers and Constables are hereby instructed to prevent the entrance into the Meadow of all beggars. all persons in ragged or very dirty clothes.persons of improper character or who are not decent in appearance and behaviour: and to prevent indecent . rude . or disorderly conduct of every description .

To allow no handcarts . wheelbarrows . no hawkers or persons carrying parcels or bundles so as to obstruct the walks.

To prevent the flying of kites. throwing stones. throwing balls. bowling hoops. shooting arrows. firing guns or pistols. or playing games attended with danger or inconvenience to passers-by: also fishing in the waters. catching birds. bird-nesting or cycling.

To prevent all persons cutting names on. breaking or injuring the seats. shrubs.plants. trees or turf.

To prevent the fastening of boats or rafts to the iron palisading or river wall and to prevent encroachments of every kind by the river-side.

THE GATES WILL CLOSE **7·30 P.M**

This quaintly worded sign in Christ Church Meadow was unfortunately replaced a few years ago.

Many **College Gardens** are superb variations on what a garden can be. There are few places in the world able to offer such a feast. See particularly Magdalen College (page 26), New College (page 34), St John's College (page 40), and Worcester College (page 45) but make your own discoveries, even if some of them will be tantalizing glimpses through locked gates.

Those of a moping, romantic disposition might like to try the **burial grounds** at Holywell, adjacent to the church of St Cross (map →F2), whose illustrious dead include Kenneth Grahame, author of *Wind in the Willows* (see page 76), or St Sepulchre's off Walton Street (map →B1).

Or for something different, try a **Canal** walk and look at the fascinating customized and decorated houseboats moored alongside the towpath starting at Hythe Bridge Street (map →B3) and running north. If you feel energetic you can keep going to Banbury. It's only 43 kilometres (27 miles).

Food, Drink (and Music)

The Dodo was reputed to take pebbles into its gizzard to aid digestion. You should be able to do better than that in Oxford without attempting to emulate the feats of earlier generations, such as draining a bottle of port out of a fox's head. Oxford is a romantic city and music is the food of love so we have lumped it into this section too.

The first coffee-house in England opened on Oxford's High Street in 1650—you can take a cup on the same spot today, at the Grand Café, 84 High Street.

Eating is too serious a business for us to do it justice within this small book, so we are restricting ourselves to light refreshments and snacks. Places you may like to try are **The Nosebag** in St Michael's Street, and the Medieval ambience of coffee house and restaurant that is part of **St Mary's Church** on the Radcliffe Square side. There are also the cafés at the **Ashmolean Museum** on Beaumont Street and **Modern Art Oxford**, the popular brasserie **Browns** on Woodstock Road just beyond St Giles, or perhaps you could push the boat out by taking afternoon tea and cakes at the **Randolph Hotel** in Beaumont Street. There are coffee shops everywhere, including those in the main bookshops, and concentrations of bars, restaurants, and cafés on George Street, the High Street, Gloucester Green, on Walton Street, and the Cowley Road.

THE COVERED MARKET (entered from High Street or Market Street) has colourful displays of food to feast your eyes on, as well as cafés (at **Brown's**—not the same one as this has the apostrophe—you can try 'dripping toast'), tea and coffee specialists, delicatessens, and a specialist sausage shop for your Oxford Sausages or 'dainties'. Another entrance to the Market is from Cornmarket via **The Golden Cross**—a shopping development made out of the courtyard of an ancient inn. In **Pizza Express** you can see 16th-century wall paintings restored during the renovation.

In Oxford's cafés and restaurants you may find yourself amongst some odd-looking people talking about the strangest things. Don't worry, they're probably just very intelligent.

PUBS Alcohol is of course a food but most pubs will sell various kinds of solid stuff alongside their Old Speckled Hen, Old Peculiar, etc. **The Turf** pub is discovered down St Helen's Passage from New College Lane or Bath Place from Holywell Street, nestled against part of the old city wall. Nearby **The King's Arms**, on the corner of Broad Street and Holywell Street, is very popular with students, who spill themselves and their drinks over the surrounding pavements. **The Bear**, on the corner of Alfred and Blue Boar Streets, is famous for its collection of ties that line the walls and ceilings, while **The Eagle and Child** at 49 St Giles (known affectionately as *The Bird and Babe*) was a regular haunt of *The Inklings* (see page 77). Further afield are the thatched **Perch** at Binsey, and **The Trout** at Wolvercote.

MUSIC Oxford has always been a musical city and made something of a reputation as a breeding-ground for new bands with the emergence of Radiohead and Supergrass in the 1990s. To discover where to go and what's on, get hold of *Nightshift*, a free monthly magazine (www.nightshift. oxfordmusic.net). Some of the liveliest venues include *The Zodiac*, 190 Cowley Road (www.zodiac.co.uk), the *Wheat-sheaf*, 129 High Street, and *Port Mahon*, 82 St Clements (www.portmahon.co.uk) for more folk sounds. If your tastes are more genteel there are regular concerts and recitals at the Sheldonian Theatre and Holywell Music Room, in Holywell Street. Check the posters outside these buildings or visit the Playhouse Theatre box office (telephone 798600) where tickets can usually be bought, or try Music at Oxford (www.musicatoxford.com, telephone 0870 7500659). There are often choral and instrumental recitals in college chapels and Oxford Town Hall. Also check out the Oxford Informa-tion Centre in Broad Street, or Daily Information posters (www.dailyinfo.co.uk).

Alexander Nowell, Principal of Brasenose College (1507–1602) is credited with the invention of bottled beer. A keen fisherman, he left a bottle of ale on the river bank and return-ing 'found it . . . no bottle but a gun'.

William Buckland, a geologist at Christ Church (1784–1856) reckoned he'd eaten his way through the entire animal kingdom, the nastiest things being a mole, or perhaps a bluebottle. Did he try Dodo?

Bicycles in Oxford

The golden age of cycling was probably at the end of the 19th century. Innovations like ball bearings, pneumatic tyres, knickerbockers, and bloomers gave devotees of the new craze undreamt of comfort and freedom, so long as they ignored the publication Cycling as a Cause of Heart Disease *by a senior physician. Oxford still has masses of two-wheeled traffic. Take care as you wander, eyes aloft, across pedestrianized streets; you might be mown down by a speeding cyclist!*

Students exploit bikes as cheap, convenient, low-maintenance transport, conveying them on their many short journeys at—according to the theory— three or four times the speed of a pedestrian and using five times less energy in the process. Parking isn't a problem: they shackle their bike to any handy railing, lamp post, or drainpipe, or pile them in tangled heaps against college walls, as you will see in, for instance, Turl Street. The evidence seems to be that it's worth arriving late if you want to stand a chance of making a quick getaway. Most students seem to buy secondhand and sell on, while some hire by the term. Up to 3,000 bikes get stolen every year, but the cycles department at the main police station reckons to return eight out of ten to its owner, the unclaimed being auctioned or sold off, raising £5000 to £6000 a year. Oxford once had a system of distinctively coloured bikes that you

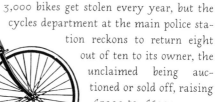

could pick up and leave as you needed, free of charge. This didn't last long—too many disappeared.

There has always been guerilla warfare between bikes and other traffic in Oxford. Both sides accuse the other of recklessness and arrogance. Things were not always so bad

… and here is the same bike returning.

tempered. In 1876 students were advised: If a horse, on meeting a bicycle, shows signs of restiveness, it is not always wise to dismount at once. To dismount suddenly is more likely to frighten a horse than to continue riding slowly by, talking to the horse as you do so. Oxford has made great efforts to minimise friction with cycle lanes and cycle-only routes from north and south of the city into the centre. Leaflets are available at the Oxford Information Centre.

Bike Shops such as *Warlands* (established 1906) at 63 Botley Road, near the railway station, will sell or hire you a bike, repair it, and accessorize it for you. You might like a folding one, or one of those with a little front wheel and whopping basket that delivery boys ride. Other bike shops include *Bikezone* on Market Street, *Beeline Bikes* on Cowley Road, and *Walton Street Cycles* (on Walton Street!).

If the motor car became the scourge of the cyclist and put an end to its golden age, then **William Morris** embodied the transition. He began his career in 1893 at the age of sixteen by opening his own bicycle repair shop at the back of his father's house in east Oxford after being refused a 1 shilling a week rise at his first job. He was a formidable cyclist, the local champion at distances from one to fifty miles by 1900. But he moved on to cars, and became the biggest manufacturer in the country by 1926, became Viscount Nuffield, and donated £27 million to the University.

The much-loved Mini, a classic design of 1959 by Alec Issigonis, was in continuous production for forty years and named car of the century. Since 2001 a newly designed Mini has been made at Cowley, the Oxford suburb where Morris opened his car factory in 1913. A Mr John Evans was able to balance one of the original Minis weighing 160kg, or 352lbs, on his head for thirty three seconds.

John Betjeman on the romance of cycling:

Shall we ever, my staunch Myfanwy,
Bicycle down to North Parade?
Kant on the handle-bars, Marx in the saddlebag,
Light my touch on your shoulder-blade.

The Dodo Walk

Here's a leisurely circular walk I'd like to take you on, around some of the smaller streets and alleyways of Oxford. It will give you a chance to get away from the busier tourist spots and have a look at everyday life. My pace is of necessity, given my years and modest stature, somewhat sedate, so if you wish to push on, the route is clearly marked on the map on pages 94–95. It starts and ends opposite the Emperors in Broad Street, between Blackwell's Bookshop and the New Bodleian Library, and takes at least an hour.

Here are a few things to watch out for:

- The route of the walk runs close to the boundary of the old city wall, so will give you a feel for the size and shape of Medieval Oxford, before it began to expand into the surrounding countryside during the 17th century (about the time man's unstoppable expansion led to the extinction of my fellow birds in the far away Indian Ocean).

- Refreshment is available on the route at interesting old pubs. The Turf Tavern is tucked up under a surviving section of the city wall, but it's too soon to be stopping already, unless you are doing the walk in a counter–clockwise direction. Then there is the Bear Inn on Bear Lane with its famous collection of ties, displayed on the walls and ceiling, begun by the landlord in 1952. Modern Art Oxford in Pembroke Street has coffee and food as well as culture, there's the Nosebag restaurant in St Michael's Street, and sandwich shops in Ship Street.

- Cobbles occur now and again, a little painful for my dainty feet, but attractive. How important the preservation of things like roads, pavements, walls, and trees are, as well as the buildings, for the whole experience of Oxford. Merton Street is the last sizeable street in the city to keep its cobbles, and these are protected by grade II listing.

- The colleges and university buildings occupy plenty of space in Oxford, but keep your eyes open and you'll see many less obvious buildings that have been taken over. In Pembroke Street for instance there are some old houses made into student accommodation that look a bit sad for losing the use of their front doors.

- A lot of the time you won't be able to wander where you'd like because much of Oxford is private and some colleges, like University College, keep visitors out. All you can see of it is a tantalising glimpse through a side gate in Logic Lane (if it is open) and the front gate in the High Street. And as Queen's College only admits guided parties (I don't count, apparently) there's just the view into the front quad.

- Our route shows short-cuts and quieter byways, used by Oxford's students, workers, and shoppers. Watch out crossing the busier roads though, the High Street and St Aldate's in particular. One of the stronger members of the party might like to give me a lift across the road. Much obliged.

- There might be an opportunity to watch Real Tennis being played, an ancient but not quite extinct game. The court is on Merton Street, on the opposite side from Merton College. Look out for a set-back shop-like entrance and ask.

- Keep looking up. Many of the most interesting sights are above eye-level, like the carved ugly heads on New College in New College Lane, or the interesting things that grow on the top of walls, or the trees that peer over them. Or even higher, like the golden elephant weather vane on the Indian Institute. So look up, but don't trip up.

- Watch out for the house in Oriel Square, traditionally painted a provocative colour. Currently it is a sort of pink.

- Let me know if you find anything better than a low wall to perch on. There's a distinct shortage of seats and my short legs get tired.

Beyond Oxford

Oxford is not just a university, or even a county town. It is the capital of Oxfordshire, with lovely varied countryside all around, and if your stay is for more than a few days it would be a shame not to explore beyond the ring road. There's no need to go too far—after all, your guide the Dodo's range is somewhat restricted by his physical attributes.

BLENHEIM PALACE Don't turn your nose up at this just because it's the most obvious trip out of Oxford. You would have to be someone quite unusual not to be impressed. It's the biggest private house in the country, home to the Duke of Marlborough, whose ancestor was awarded the land and money to build the palace by Queen Anne after his defeat of the French at the Battle of Blenheim in 1704. The scale of it is stupendous, from the richly decorated rooms, to the sweeping grounds laid out by Capability Brown; although the room in which Winston Churchill was born is actually quite modest. You can walk for miles around the lakes and through the woods, get lost in the maze, dawdle in the butterfly house and flower gardens, or take a ride on the miniature railway. Take the number 20 bus from the Gloucester Green bus station. Once you are in Woodstock the best approach to the palace is via Park Street through the town centre (follow the signs) to the triumphal arch and an unforgettable view. The park is open all year 9am-5pm, the palace mid-March to the end of October, 10.30am-5.30pm.

If you like houses and gardens, try **Rousham House** (18th-century), **Broughton Castle** (Medieval), **Waterperry garden and nursery**, **Chastleton House** (Jacobean), **Kelmscott Manor** (home of the Pre-Raphaelite, William Morris), and **Minster Lovell**

Hall (a beautiful riverside ruin). You will need your own transport for these, and can get directions from the Oxford Information Centre in Broad Street.

Every summer there are a number of excellent college productions of Shakespeare's plays, but you may wish to pay homage to 'The Bard' at source, by going to **Stratford-upon-Avon** and one of the Royal Shakespeare Company theatres.

Much closer to Oxford is **Iffley village**, only three kilometres (two miles) from the centre. It's been enveloped by the growing city, but remains unspoilt and has one of the most magnificent Norman churches in England, its doors and windows ornamented with zig-zags, rows of beakheads, signs of the zodiac, and fantastic beasts. Take a bus from the High Street, or if you are feeling fit, walk along the towpath from Folly Bridge past the university boathouses, Iffley lock and weirs, and the handy riverside pub **The Isis**.

Those of you yearning for the quintessential pretty English village could try **Great Tew**. It has all the right ingredients, including a famous pub, The Falkland Arms (10 kilometres or 6 miles east of Chipping Norton, off the B4022, no public transport). For something a little more natural go to **Ewelme**, on the fringes of the Chilterns (3 kilometres or 2 miles east of Benson, off the B4009, no public transport) which has a memorable grouping of Medieval church, school, and almshouses (the charitable gift of Alice, the granddaughter of Geoffrey Chaucer, who lost three husbands, three grandsons, and one brother-in-law to war and violence and lies in alabaster effigy under an elaborate canopy in the church).

If you want to look at a country town, **Burford** is small and beautiful, with its eminently strollable High Street of handsome Cotswold stone buildings dropping steeply down to the river. There is a wealth of shops, cafés, pubs, and antique shops along this street, and just off it is the grand Medieval church of St John the Baptist. If Burford is definitely geared to the tourist trade, **Abingdon** (you can travel there by Salter's river boats in the summer, www.salterbros.fsnet.co.uk, telephone 01865 243421) or **Chipping Norton**, have more bustle and variety.

Artweeks is the visual arts festival for Oxfordshire, and usually takes place in May and June. Many hundreds of artists and makers open up their studios to show their work. The website is www.artweeks.org

If you fancy a trip up to **London**, you can go by train or by either of the two coach companies that run from Gloucester Green Coach and Bus Station.

Credits

This guidebook reproduces many of the wonderful illustrations by the 19th-century artist engravers, John Tenniel and Orlando Jewitt. Lewis Carroll, the author of *Alice's Adventures in Wonderland* and *Through the Looking-Glass* first contacted Orlando Jewitt, one of the finest engravers of architectural illustrate his books with some wonderful images that add so much to the text. Looking-Glass eventually had John Tenniel and topographical views of

his day, to illustrate his *Alice* book, although Jewitt's work was not used in the end. Jewitt illustrated many of the works of the leaders of the Gothic Revival, such as A. W. N. Pugin, Sir Gilbert Scott, and G. E. Street. Jewitt's engravings of Oxford shown in this guidebook were usually based on drawings made by W. A. Delamotte, and were originally created for the three volume *Memorials of Oxford* published in the 1830s. It was perhaps the high-point in Jewitt's career.

Carroll and Tenniel had a rather strained working relationship, for example Carroll only liked one of the ninety two drawings Tenniel made—an engraving of Humpty Dumpty. Relations became so bad that despite the success of *Alice's Adventures in Wonderland*, it took two and a half years before Tenniel was persuaded to illustrate the second *Alice* book. The brothers Edward and George Dalziel engraved Tenniel's drawings.

In 1865 two thousand copies of *Alice's Adventures in Wonderland* were printed by the Clarendon Press in Oxford, but Tenniel was so dissatisfied with the pictures that it was reprinted by Richard Clay in London, at a cost to Carroll of £600. Only a handful of the first 'rejected' edition survive and are now worth a small fortune.

The other drawings, including the Oxford dodos, are copyright of Dodo Publishing. For the critical read of the text we appreciate the help, in particular, of William Clennell, Edith Gollnast, Malcolm Graham, Margaret Williamson, and the various colleges and university institutions that kindly checked their entries.

The authors would like to thank friends and family who helped in the creation of this guidebook, and of course, our friend the Oxford Dodo.

Maps of Oxford

The tradition in Oxford was for maps to be arranged
so that they look from the north towards the south.
Sadly, this topsy-turvy approach has fallen out of favour
in recent years. It was tempting to reintroduce it, but
you might well have found that you were walking in
entirely the wrong direction! This probably would not have
been such a bad thing as it is often the best way to
discover a place. Instead we have followed convention,
with north at the top of the page. The maps that follow
show progressively more detail.

"You are old," said the youth, "as I mentioned before,
And have grown most uncommonly fat;
Yet you turned a back-somersault in at the door—
Pray, what is the reason of that?"

Car parking in Oxford is both difficult and expensive, so it is normal to use one of the five 'Park & Ride' **bus** sites. You park your car and travel into the centre of Oxford using the frequent bus service. These sites are shown by the **P&R** symbol on the map opposite.

If you need to park a **car** in the city centre then there is some metered roadside parking, such as on St Giles, as well as the car parks marked by a **P** on the maps on pages 92–95.

The mainline **Railway station** is on the Botley Road (see the map opposite, and on page 92, **→A3**), and the **Coach and Bus station** in Gloucester Green (see the map opposite, and on page 92, **→C3**). These have frequent services to London and elsewhere.

Organized **coach tours** usually make use of the Oxpens Coach Park next to the ice rink, (see the map on page 92, **→B5**).

GETTING TO OXFORD

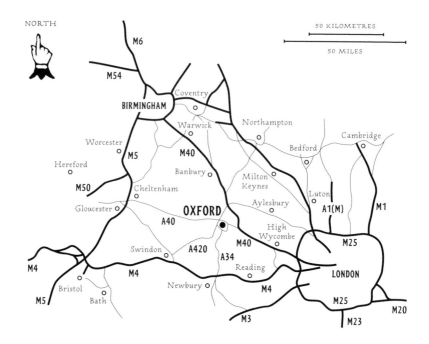

OXFORD AND THE RING ROAD

NORTH

*See the next page
for an enlargement
of this area.*

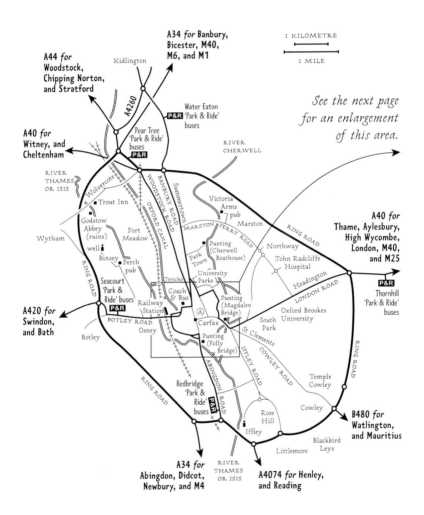

A34 *for* Banbury,
Bicester, M40,
M6, and M1

A44 *for*
Woodstock,
Chipping Norton,
and Stratford

Kidlington

A4260

Water Eaton
P&R 'Park & Ride'
buses

A40 *for*
Witney, and
Cheltenham

Pear Tree
'Park & Ride'
buses
P&R

RIVER
CHERWELL

1 KILOMETRE

1 MILE

RIVER
THAMES
OR ISIS

Wolvercote

■ Trout Inn

WOODSTOCK CANAL

BANBURY ROAD

OXFORD CANAL

Summertown

Victoria
Arms
¬ pub

A40 *for*
Thame, Aylesbury,
High Wycombe,
London, M40,
and M25

Godstow
Abbey
(ruins)

Wytham

well ■

Port
Meadow

MARSTON FERRY ROAD

Marston

RING ROAD

Binsey ■

Perch
pub

Punting
(Cherwell
Boathouse)

Northway

John Radcliffe
Hospital

Park
Town

Seacourt
'Park &
Ride' buses
P&R

Jericho

University
Parks

Headington

LONDON ROAD

Railway
Station

Coach
& Bus

Punting
(Magdalen
Bridge)

Oxford Brookes
University

P&R

Thornhill
'Park & Ride'
buses

A420 *for*
Swindon,
and Bath

BOTLEY ROAD

Ⓐ

Carfax ■

South
Park

Botley

Osney

St Clements

Punting
(Folly
Bridge)

RING ROAD

RING ROAD

ABINGDON ROAD

IFFLEY ROAD

COWLEY ROAD

Temple
Cowley

Redbridge
'Park &
Ride'
buses
P&R

Rose
Hill

Cowley

B480 *for*
Watlington,
and Mauritius

Iffley ■

Blackbird
Leys

Littlemore

A34 *for*
Abingdon, Didcot,
Newbury, and M4

RIVER
THAMES
OR ISIS

A4074 *for* Henley,
and Reading

OXFORD

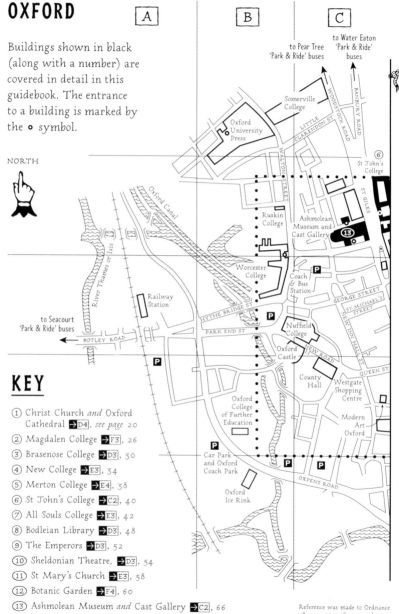

Buildings shown in black
(along with a number) are
covered in detail in this
guidebook. The entrance
to a building is marked by
the o symbol.

NORTH

KEY

1. Christ Church *and* Oxford
   Cathedral **D4**, *see page* 20
2. Magdalen College **F3**, 26
3. Brasenose College **D3**, 30
4. New College **E3**, 34
5. Merton College **E4**, 38
6. St John's College **C2**, 40
7. All Souls College **E3**, 42
8. Bodleian Library **D3**, 48
9. The Emperors **D3**, 52
10. Sheldonian Theatre, **D3**, 54
11. St Mary's Church **E3**, 58
12. Botanic Garden **F4**, 60
13. Ashmolean Museum *and* Cast Gallery **C2**, 66
14. University Museum of Natural History
    and the Pitt Rivers Museum **D1**, 68

Reference was made to Ordnance
Survey maps of 1937 and 1939
in the production of this map.

© Dodo Publishing

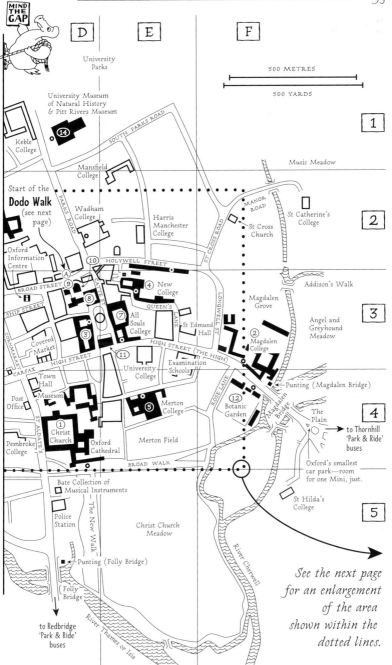

CITY CENTRE

The entrance to a building is marked by the o symbol.

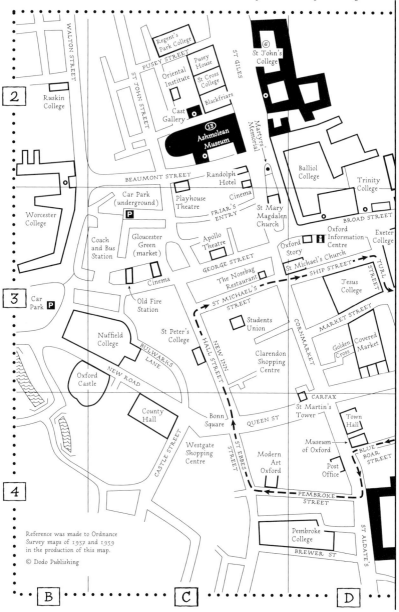

Reference was made to Ordnance
Survey maps of 1937 and 1939
in the production of this map.

© Dodo Publishing

The **Dodo walk** around the centre of Oxford (see page 84) is shown below with a dashed line. It begins and ends at point Ⓐ on Broad Street, which is between Blackwell's Bookshop and the New Bodleian Library.

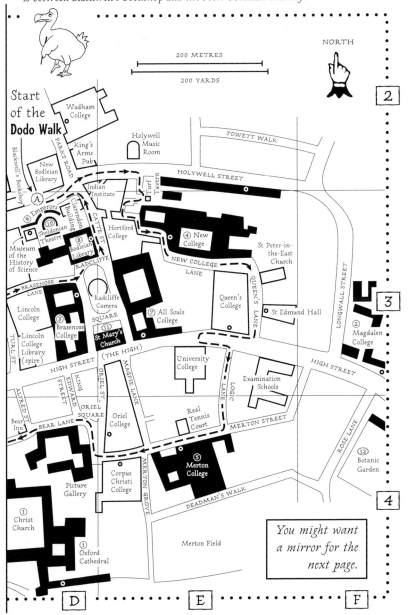

200 METRES

200 YARDS

NORTH

Start of the **Dodo Walk**

Wadham College

Holywell Music Room

King's Arms Pub

JOWETT WALK

Blackwell's Bookshop

New Bodleian Library

PARKS ROAD

Indian Institute

HOLYWELL STREET

Turf Tavern

Emperor's

Clarendon Building

CATTE ST.

Hertford College

④ New College

St Peter-in-the-East Church

⑨

⑩

Sheldonian Theatre

⑧ Bodleian Library

RADCLIFFE

NEW COLLEGE LANE

Museum of the History of Science

BRASENOSE LANE

Radcliffe Camera

SQUARE

Queen's College

QUEEN'S LANE

LONGWALL STREET

Lincoln College

③ Brasenose College

⑪ St Mary's Church

⑦ All Souls College

St Edmund Hall

② Magdalen College

③

TURL ST.

Lincoln College Library (spire)

HIGH STREET

(THE HIGH)

University College

LOGIC LANE

HIGH STREET

ALFRED ST.

KING EDWARD STREET

ORIEL ST.

MAGPIE LANE

Examination Schools

Bear Inn

ORIEL SQUARE

BEAR LANE

Oriel College

Real Tennis Court

MERTON STREET

ROSE LANE

MERTON GROVE

⑤ **Merton College**

⑫ Botanic Garden

Picture Gallery

Corpus Christi College

① Christ Church

① Oxford Cathedral

DEADMAN'S WALK

Merton Field

You might want a mirror for the next page.

2

3

4

D   E   F

The Dodo Guide to
OXFORD

Philip Atkins &
Michael Johnson

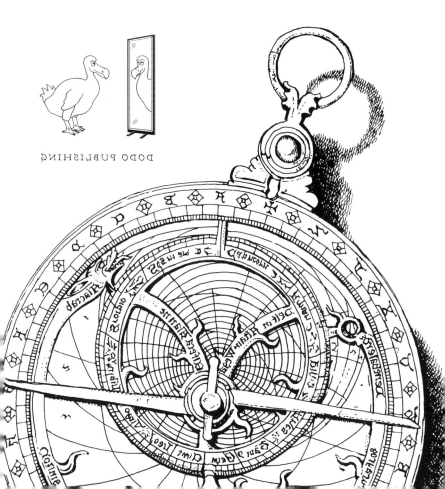

DODO PUBLISHING